How to Get Promoted
Keys to Getting Ahead in Life
by Michael Fletcher

How to Get Promoted
Copyright © 2007 by Michael Fletcher
ISBN 978-1-60461-620-0

Published by
Advance the Kingdom Publishing
5117 Cliffdale Rd.
Fayetteville, NC 28314
910-867-9151

All scriptures references from:

The Holy Bible: New International Version (NIV), Copyright © 1973, 1978, 1984 by International Bible Society. All Rights Reserved

The Holy Bible: New King James Version (NKJV) Copyright © 1979, 1980, 1982 by Thomas Nelson Inc. All Rights Reserved.

1 2 3 4 5 6 7 8 9 / 07 08 09 10

Contents

Introduction
31 Leaders, Career Makers and Career Breakers

I am a pastor, and a pastor's job is more than just teaching the Bible. Our calling is to help people live better lives. That includes teaching the Bible, of course, but it requires us to seek ways to apply those truths to the everyday lives of the people we serve. We are called first to help them answer the most important question in life and settle the "heaven and hell issue." Then, we are called to teach them how to live and more than that, how to succeed at life – how to have relationships that last, how to have marriages that are still fused with romance after forty years, how to train children who are respectful and grow up with a desire to stay close and connected with family, how to live a life that impacts others and makes a difference in the world.

A huge portion of a person's life is spent at work. I am not even taking into account the years spent in preparation for work in terms of schooling. Nor am I calculating the hundreds of hours spent commuting to and from the place of business. A healthy 8-hours-a-day, five-days-a-week employee with two weeks vacation and six paid holidays spends 1952 hours at work per year! That is a huge chunk of life! But these are more than just hours burned. This is how that employee funds his/her life. Where he/she lives, what he/she drives, where his/her children go to school is all determined in large part by that job. Everything about his/her socio-economic lifestyle is shaped by what happens at work. Not only that, the place of work and how an employee feels about going to that place greatly impacts his/her emotional well-being, which affects all the relationships around him. Work is clearly important!

If people are going to live successful lives, work is going to be a big part of the equation. Does the Bible have anything to say about being successful at work? Tons! But once again, Bible truth needs to be couched in very practical terms if we are really going to help people live better lives. We can't just teach their heads to know Bible facts. We have to empower them with hands-on application – stuff they can take home and take to work to help them build a better tomorrow.

The Bible is an amazing book and accurate in every way – historically, scientifically, spiritually. Everything you need for life and godliness is in this Book – how to find a great spouse, how to rear fantastic children, how to go to heaven when you die, how to run a business or even a country, and how to get promoted.

I knew I could comb the pages of Scripture and find out what God had to say about how to get promoted, how to get ahead in life, but I decided to take another approach. I started first with business leaders, entrepreneurs, pastors, and military leaders, both male and female, and conducted my own private survey over a period of several months. The people I surveyed are people who are successful in their own right, but more than that, these are the people who decide who else gets ahead in life and who does not – career "makers" and career "breakers." I wanted to know what they thought. What do they look for in an employee? What, in their minds, determines who gets promoted and who gets passed over?

What traits are they looking for in employees they put forward? What kinds of things hold a person back? I am grateful to the 31 leaders who spent hours putting their thoughts together in an effort to help me help you.

Don't get me wrong, I did not neglect the Scriptures. Just the opposite, I knew that these folks would not create new ideas for God, but simply confirm those already tucked in the pages of the Bible.

This book is the result of that survey. Again, let me reiterate, this is not a theoretical exposition of some lofty, unattainable ideals. This is practical, horse-sense type stuff, the kind of stuff you can take home and put to use, stuff than can help you get ahead in life.

At the end of each chapter are some "reflection questions." These can be used individually or in a small group setting. Either way, do not neglect to give your attention to these. They help you create or identify your personal "take-away" ideas from each chapter. You want to get ahead, right? These questions are designed to enable you "mine" the truths that will help make that possible!

The Number One Quality
(Many Claim to Have it But Few Really Do)

It has often been said that we tend to promote people to the level of their incompetence. Why is that? Do leaders in education, business, law enforcement, and the military really lack the common sense to recognize good employees? Why do they sometimes take the very best teacher in the school and put her in a position to be a less than average principal? Why do they sometimes take the best worker off the floor and place them in an office where they make a lousy boss?

What are they thinking! What selection criteria did they use? Faithfulness – they promoted the most "faithful" people. It seemed a "no brainer!" Who wouldn't move such a person to the next level? He was our most faithful employee. She was our most faithful teacher. But did they really promote the most "faithful" person? The idea is great but the definition is often wrong.

Chapter One

Faithfulness

Being Able to Improve the Circumstances
You Have Been Handed

Mildred worked in the nursery at church for years. She
had been in charge of it now for the last six years. She had become
what some might call the "Nursery Nazi." She ran things with an
iron fist. It was her way or the highway. But everybody had got-
ten used to that. It had been her way for the last six years. In fact,
nothing had really changed in that time – the colors of wall and
carpet, the decorations that adorned the walls, the set up of the
room, the policies and procedures that governed the place – all the
same.

Finally, Mildred "retired." Since there was no pay she didn't actually retire as in "collect a monthly retirement check." Actually, for
some unknown reason, she just quit. She wasn't mad; she was just
done. People, especially the pastor, outwardly mourned the loss
but inwardly they cheered. For six years every new idea had been
rejected; every new enthusiastic worker had been run off; every
hint toward change had been stubbornly resisted. And now, she
was gone – not out of the church, just out of the nursery.

The task fell to Pastor Smith to appoint a new nursery chief. Pastor Smith was known to be a thoughtful and wise man. He had made a careful study of human nature over his many years of ministry and had trained untold numbers of leaders. He was equal to the task. And the task was simple. Mildred the "Nursery Nazi" had been flanked for most of these last six years by a woman of saintly character named Henrietta.

Henrietta was the picture of faithfulness. She was there every week without fail. If vacation or sickness prohibited her from fulfilling her weekly duty she made sure to call a suitable substitute. And she consistently abided by the nursery policies – never wavered. Things had to be a certain way and she made sure to follow the order and stay in line. She was easily number two in the chain of command. She knew the system. She was always there. She deserved a shot at number one. She was next – an easy pick.

Pastor Smith acted wisely in not appointing a new nursery coordinator too soon. People needed time to recognize the loss of Mildred. She needed to be missed. He would wait to the end of the month and appoint Henrietta. Everyone, even Mildred, would applaud the move. Wise Pastor Smith once again leads the church with insight. If only all the problems in the church were this easily handled!

Jennifer had only been in the church less than a year. She served her rotation in the nursery like every other good mother in the church. But in the last three months she had become increasingly burdened to serve the children. She began to volunteer often. She wasn't really clear about all the details concerning policy and procedure – wasn't really her thing. What made her "tick" was simply love for the kids.

Ten days after Mildred's resignation, the pastor swings by the church building to pick up the Saturday mail. Walking through the building, he runs into Jennifer who immediately began to apologize.

"I'm sorry for the mess. I promise it will be all cleaned up for Sunday morning service. And as for the painting, my husband and I will get to that right after church – wouldn't want that strong paint odor while the kids are in here in the morning." She led the pastor into the nursery where her husband had just finished affixing the new changing station to the wall.

"That old changing station was too far from the check-in. Sometimes when you are in here all alone, it is difficult to give adequate care to the babies and serve the mothers checking in kids at the same time. We want the best care for the babies, and we want to give good "customer service" to the moms as well. People should not have to wait to check in their kids. Besides, the old changing station looked dilapidated. We hated to think what the visitors thought when they saw it. We knew there were no church funds for a new one – Mildred told us that – so my husband and I bought a new one, the best one, from the church supply company along with some new paint to match the hallway and some new bright wall decorations. This will make the place more desirable to the children and help us provide families with the best of care. Not to mention it brings the nursery into line with the decor on the rest of the property. I 'm sorry we won't get the painting done before tomorrow."

Pastor Smith thanked them profusely, blown away by their initiative, creativity, and generosity. He couldn't believe the place! On the way home, Pastor Smith began to rehearse the agenda for tomorrow which included a short meeting after church with Henrietta where he would appoint her the new nursery coordinator. The "Nursery Nazi" regime would continue with a new name and new face. Henrietta would be nicer than Mildred, but the same mentality would rule and nothing would change – for at least another six years.

Reader, tell me honestly. Who would you want in charge of the nursery if you attended that church? Your heart says, "Jennifer," but your mind argues for Henrietta. And your main point? She served faithfully for almost six years. Did she really? Was she faithful or just consistent?

The Bible wisely speaks to the issue in Proverbs 20:6 (NASB) "Many a man proclaims his own loyalty, but a faithful man who can find?" Have you ever met someone who openly admits they are not faithful? Everyone thinks of himself as being faithful. The real question lies in the definition of "faithful."

A conventional definition of "faithful" might include thoughts like – dependable, consistent, a person who retains what they have been given, a person who shows up for work and does the same job the same way over a long period of time.

Using this definition, longevity plays a major role in getting ahead in life – getting promoted. And that is why we tend to promote people to their level of incompetence. Employers know no other way and see no other options. Let's try another definition, the biblical one, one that, if you embrace this quality and make it your own, will separate you from the crowd and give your employer the person he/she has been looking for!

A biblical definition of faithfulness might be as follows: Use all that you have been given to improve the circumstances you have been handed. The story at the beginning of this chapter illustrates the point. Henrietta would be just more of the same – nothing would improve, all would stay the same. "You aren't giving her a chance!" She had almost six years to demonstrate faithfulness. Instead, she showed great consistency (and she should be commended for that) but very little real faithfulness. Jennifer on the other hand, is a picture of faithfulness. She sought to improve the circumstances she was handed. She tried to take things to the next level.

Employers aren't looking for people to hold down the fort and collect a check. They want employees who put their hearts into it, people who come to work everyday seeking not only to improve but also to make improvements! When you are faithful – using all that you have been given to improve the circumstances you have been handed – you cannot help but stand out. "Many a man proclaims his own loyalty (everyone talks a good game), but a faithful man who can find (very few actually come through)?"

Listen to this parable from the teaching of Jesus found in Matthew 25:14-29 (NIV) [14]"Again, it will be like a man going on a journey, who called his servants and entrusted his property to them. [15]To one he gave five talents of money, to another two talents, and to another one talent, each according to his ability. Then he went on his journey. [16]The man who had received the five talents went at once and put his money to work and gained five more. [17]So also, the one with the two talents gained two more. [18]But the man who had received the one talent went off, dug a hole in the ground and hid his master's money.

[19]"After a long time the master of those servants returned and settled accounts with them. 20The man who had received the five talents brought the other five. 'Master,' he said, 'you entrusted me with five talents. See, I have gained five more.'

[21]"His master replied, 'Well done, good and faithful servant! You have been faithful with a few things; I will put you in charge of many things. Come and share your master's happiness!'

[22]"The man with the two talents also came. 'Master,' he said, 'you entrusted me with two talents; see, I have gained two more.'

[23]"His master replied, 'Well done, good and faithful servant! You have been faithful with a few things; I will put you in charge of many things. Come and share your master's happiness!'

[24]"Then the man who had received the one talent came. 'Master,' he said, 'I knew that you are a hard man, harvesting where you have not sown and gathering where you have not scattered seed.

²⁵So I was afraid and went out and hid your talent in the ground. See, here is what belongs to you.'

²⁶"His master replied, 'You wicked, lazy servant! So you knew that I harvest where I have not sown and gather where I have not scattered seed? ²⁷Well then, you should have put my money on deposit with the bankers, so that when I returned I would have received it back with interest.

²⁸"'Take the talent from him and give it to the one who has the ten talents. ²⁹For everyone who has will be given more, and he will have an abundance. Whoever does not have, even what he has will be taken from him.'"

Permit some observations:

1. Both the recipient of the five talents and the two talents receive the same reward and were promoted. Why? Jesus says twice in verse 21 and twice again in verse 23 that these men are faithful. He stresses that. And how is that determination made? They improved the lot they had been handed.

2. The other fellow in the story holds on to his portion – doesn't lose a thing – and he is called wicked and lazy. Why? By today's definition he was faithful. He held on to what he had been given. He was dependable. He was a same-job-done-the-same-way kind of guy. By Jesus definition he wasn't faithful. And he lost what he had.

3. The employee with 10 talents gets the one talent taken from the employee deemed unfaithful. Why give it to him? Because the employer is interested in increase. Why not make things more equal and give it to the guy with 4 talents? Simple. Both men had the capacity and work ethic to double what they had been given. 4 talents + 1 talent = 5 talents. Double that and you get 10 talents. 10 talents + 1 talent = 11 talents. Double that and you get 22 talents!

The lesson is clear. Faithful people get ahead. This is the #1 quality employers are looking for. The company you work for does not exist to provide you a paycheck. It exists to make a profit, to accomplish a mission or to fulfill a task. The leaders of that company, unit, or organization are focused on developing a work-force to accomplish that goal. They are looking for men and women to help labor with them toward that end. Are you that person? Are you who they are looking for? Not if you are a do-the-same-thing-the same-way kind of employee! If you want to go to the next level, go to the next level tomorrow. Take your job up a notch – improve your circumstances. Get there early. Look around. Think. Pray. Put your heart into it – not just to get promoted, but to demonstrate the kind of person you really are. "Many a man proclaims his own loyalty, but a faithful man who can find?" Prove you are that kind person by living that kind of lifestyle. You can't fake it long. Either you are faithful, or you are not.

You might be asking, "What should I do?" First, if you are not desirous of moving on and getting ahead in life, put this book down. What follows is some of the best advice I have seen anywhere – given by those who are in a position to make and break careers. (All I have done is catalog and compile that advice and pass it on to you.) Second, concerning the matter of faithfulness, consider the following:

1. Recognize that promotion comes from the Lord. Work for Him. Work "beyond" your earthly boss and work everyday for the Lord. If you work for God, even if your boss is a jerk or one of those people promoted to his level of incompetence, his personality or lack of it will not get in your way.
2. Review your strengths and weaknesses. Play your strengths.
3. Release the creativity of your calling in the place where you are. You have a calling on your life – a purpose for living. Creativity is embedded in that calling. Release it.

In short, be faithful – improve the circumstances you have been handed. Faithful people get ahead because faithfulness is the #1 quality employers are looking for!

Chapter One Reflection Questions:

1. What strengths do you possess? Ask those close to you to tell you what they see.

2. As painful as it may be, ask your friends and loved one to help you answer this question: What are my weaknesses?

3. What were you made to do? What is your calling in life? What is your passion? If I could do just one thing I would …

4. How can you use some of that creativity on your job or in your place of service?

5. What one thing can I do tomorrow to improve the circumstances I have been handed?

Seven Traits of People Who Get Ahead

(What Employers are Looking For)

Everyone wants to get ahead in life. No one wakes up in the morning and thinks or prays, "Today will be the first day of my ultimate demise. My trek downward into failure with all the financial, emotional, and relational pressure it brings begins now. Anguish and despair will eventually overtake me, and I will end my days unfulfilled and full of regret."

Most people dream the opposite. They picture themselves as having successful lives and all that goes with that – great marriage, wonderful kids who love and respect them, a job that is both rewarding and fulfilling, a life that others look up to. As we said in the Introduction, your manner and place of work has a lot to do with your sense of well-being. A lot of what happens in a person's life, both good and evil, is generated out of work.

So how does one get ahead at work? I asked that question to 31 individuals whose job, at least in part, is to answer that question in the lives of the people they work with and employ. I wanted to know, what do career-makers and career-breakers look for in those they promote? What traits stand out as being the most important ones and why?

Section #2 is dedicated to answering that question by outlining the "Seven Traits of People Who Get Ahead." These are the traits employers are looking for. They are, in no particular order:

1. **Passion** – Being an "Energy-Giver" Rather than an "Energy-Taker"
2. **Loyalty** – Being Committed to the Vision
3. **Integrity** – Being Able to Engender Trust from Your Employer and Co-workers
4. **Diligence** – Being Willing to Take Initiative
5. **Team Player** – Being Committed to Another's Success as Well as Your Own
6. **Emotional Intelligence** – Being Able to Relate Well with Others
7. **Teachable** – Being Willing to Learn New Things and Accept Instruction

Chapter Two

Passion
Being an "Energy-Giver" rather than an "Energy-Taker"

Numbers 14:24 (NIV) "But because my servant Caleb has a different spirit and follows me wholeheartedly, I will bring him into the land he went to, and his descendants will inherit it."

At first glance, this verse seems like a casual commendation given by God to some deserving Old Testament servant. But a look into the context provides a much more powerful picture.

The people of Israel, led at the time by Moses, refused because of their unbelief to go into the Promised Land. Caleb and his friend Joshua had been two in a party of twelve spies who surveyed the land. The other ten, intimidated by the difficulties inherent in conquering a land populated by giants living in walled cities, led the people into a rebellion generated by unbelief resulting in fear. In the end they rejected God's plan and were to live out their lives wandering in the wilderness. Worse, all those over the age of twenty would die in that wilderness and never set foot in the land – all except Joshua and Caleb.

What made Caleb different? What enabled him not only to escape the punishment of death but on that dark and sad day receive such a commendation from God Himself? God not only promised Caleb he would live, but He also promised him an inheritance in the land. Even more amazing, He promised that his descendants after him would inherit it as well. This "promotion" extended far beyond his own lifetime. Caleb and all his descendents were set for life!

The verse says that Caleb had a "different spirit" and followed God "wholeheartedly." He had passion.

I like to define "passion" as a quality that allows a person to be an "energy-giver" rather than an "energy-taker." The other ten spies were energy-takers. They sucked the life, confidence, and faith right out of the people of Israel. Caleb and his friend Joshua, however, attempted to motivate the people to be courageous and to obey the plan of God to take the land. Concerning the giants living in walled cities, Caleb boldly proclaimed, "They will be bread for us!" Forty years later, at the age of eighty-five, he made good on his words by routing the giants and inhabitants of Kirjath Arba. Not only had he been promoted, not only had this whole family been "set" for generations to come, but he fulfilled his lifelong dream in the process. Caleb "lived the life." And the key quality that positioned him to do so was passion. Through adversity, in the face of great odds, being forced to wander for half his life, even in times of war, Caleb remained an energy-giver. He had passion.

One business leader defined passion as being "sold out to the mission." For him, personal agenda, even his own has no place in his business. I listened with rapped attention as he described his mission statement. I am calling it a statement here but he read nothing to me, what he shared came out of his heart. He is looking for employees to "catch the vision" not just work for a better check. What is the vision of the company, unit, or organization you work for? That vision gives your job its purpose and meaning. If you don't know what it is, how do you know what you are working for? Or are you just working for a check? If that is the case, your employer is not looking for you. He is looking for people with passion.   Noted leadership guru John Maxwell spoke at a gathering in a city nearby. During one of his sessions I heard him say, "Successful people have an uncanny attitude toward adversity." That statement reminds me of Caleb. His passion – being sold out for the mission – enabled him to face difficult times and still dish out energy to those around him. Passion is powerful and attractive. A person with passion cannot help but be noticed, and appreciated.

I am not talking about being a "sell out" so that you violate your priorities and leave your family and friends out of your life or make them play second fiddle to your quest to get ahead. I am talking about the kind of person you are. Have you ever been around people who suck the life out of a room? You can't wait get away from them. Then there are those who emit life. You feel built up when you leave their presence. Did you know that being an energy-giver is a choice? You don't have to change your personality to become one. But you must make a daily choice.

Live like you love life; like you love people. That will translate into you living like you love your job. Even during the down days, days when everything seems to be going wrong, people who love life and who love people (energy-givers) find something that feeds them. They have an uncanny knack for being able to extract "the precious from among the rubble." Because they love life and love people, they seem to love their job; even if they don't love the job itself. Their enjoyment of the people around them and the zest for life they bring to work with them spill over into the workplace.

One military leader described passion as being contagious. "As you step up the ladder you get seen by more people. How you carry yourself, how you speak, what you say, how you react, and how you respond will be observed by all and impact those around you." Your employer has to look at how you affect the workplace. It would be irresponsible to promote someone whose attitude and actions will affect it adversely. On the other hand, it would be irresponsible NOT to promote a person of passion. Their "sold-out-for-the-mission" attitude is invaluable to the success of the organization. Truthfully, every attitude is contagious. Think again concerning the children of Israel and the ten spies. Their attitude of unbelief and fear caused a panic among the people and held them back from their promised destinies. They all fell short of their potential because of the contagious, albeit negative, influence of these men. You are contagious. The question is, what is it you are spreading? Are you giving energy or taking it?

In the same vein, a business leader said "Team members will emulate the leaders they revere. You must have an infectious enthusiasm that others with whom you work will catch." One of the things that sets a leader apart from the crowd is the ability to see the consequences associated with a set of actions. They don't just look at "now," they look at what will happen if we do this or that now. In other words, they don't just look at the action of promoting you. They look beyond that and ask, "How will promoting this person affect this company? What will be the result?" You might be answering it this way, "I'll enjoy more prestige and make more money." But the boss wants to know how promoting you will affect those around you. What affect will you have on them? Will you inspire them to "sell out" for the mission? Will your promotion make the company better or are you a dead end street? Is it that this promotion is about making your life better and you aren't really concerned about your influence on others because you aren't sold out for the mission yourself? If that is the case and you get overlooked for a post, perhaps it is because your boss isn't looking to fill a spot. She is looking to start a fire.

"You can aim a person with passion. You don't want to have

to take time to motivate a person every week." This entrepreneur is like every other leader of her ilk; she is building and creating as she goes. That is the nature of entrepreneurialism. Part of building is constructing the human infrastructure of a company – a process that is never fully complete and as the company grows, is ever changing. That means the search for good people is always on. What kind of leaders is she looking to promote? People of passion! Why? She doesn't have time to baby sit. People with passion are energy-givers, a wonderful by-product of which is being self-motivated. Once they see where they are headed, passionate people have the fuel to keep moving in that direction. Adversity and bumps in the road are viewed as challenges and often met with fresh creativity and renewed vigor; whereas those without passion (energy-takers) often view the same challenges as immovable obstacles. Those folks, under adverse circumstances tend to slow or even stop progress until the boss can give further direction or solve the problem altogether. (Remember the ten spies – immovable obstacles.) Leaders want to promote people who have the drive, the passion, the energy to press through difficulties and temporary setbacks to keep the mission on course. Those people have a future in any company!

Chapter Two Reflection Questions:

1. Are you an energy-giver or an energy-taker?
2. If you answered, "Some of both," under what circumstances do you shift from being an energy-giver to being an energy-taker?
3. You are already contagious. If your life and character were a germ, what would people be catching?
4. What qualities are present in your life that employers might like to see emulated by others?
5. Are there negative qualities in your life that your employer might view as detrimental to the organization? What are they? What do you plan to do with these?

Chapter Three

Loyalty
Being Committed to the Vision

Proverbs 14:12 (NIV) "There is a way that seems right to a man, but in the end it leads to death."

Proverbs 29:18 (KJV) "Where there is no vision, the people perish but happy is he who keeps the law."

The thing that surprised me most in my survey of these key leaders was their definition of loyalty. My personal understanding of the term is relational in nature and centers on a commitment to a person, team, or organization. Interestingly, these leaders did not define loyalty in terms of commitment to themselves as a person or to the company as an organization. To them loyalty was defined in terms of loyalty toward the mission or vision of the company, unit, or institution. "Don't just commit to who we are, commit to why we are here. Commit to what we are doing."

As I said in the last chapter, one leader defined passion as being "sold out to the mission" which prompted me to ask a question then, that I will ask again here. Have you ever read your company's mission or vision statement? If so, do you really understand its implications toward you and your job? You can't get all that a mission statement intends to say in one short reading. The people who craft these statements pour over these carefully chosen phrases with painstaking precision, grappling over the subtle nuances of each word. They are, in these statements (Some call them mission statements, others call them vision statements, still others make a big deal over the distinction between the two. I will use the terms interchangeably.) attempting to capture and communicate the essence of an organization's purpose for being. That purpose is what your boss is working toward. Are you working toward that same end?

Proverbs 29:18 says "Where there is no vision the people perish." The business cannot exist and fulfill its purpose unless the employees work in the same direction. Another version puts it this way "the people cast off restraint." In other words, when there is no vision or where the vision is unknown or ignored, the people tend to do as they please. They are unbridled and work for whatever suits them. In most cases, they simply come to work to collect a check. My guess is that the company you work for does not exist to simply provide you a paycheck. It has a purpose and, most likely, a style of doing business – accomplishing or fulfilling that purpose. The people who recognize that and who work toward that end are considered loyal in the eyes of those who lead them. If you simply work for the check, then your employer is not likely to view you as working for him/her or the company they represent. Actually, you appear to be working for yourself! You fall into the class of people who must be watched, motivated, and managed if the goals are to be fulfilled. These people are not considered loyal at all. And when it comes to promoting individuals, a key trait successful people look for in those they intend to move to the next level is loyalty!

Proverbs 29:18 ends with the phrase "but happy is he who

keeps the law." Functionally, the "law" is the moral framework that creates boundaries in life. These are the parameters in which life is to be lived. In the workplace, the "law" is defined by the mission statement. If the service department is defined by the word "quality" in the mission statement and you consistently crank out work at a higher volume than all the others but at a slightly lower level of quality, you are not likely to be a candidate for promotion. In fact, your boss may see you as a headache! You do lots of work, but the quality is not there. You think that volume is premium and often complain to your wife that you are overlooked for management positions. "It must be favoritism or office politics!" In reality, you don't know the mission and are working hard in the wrong direction. Perhaps the opposite is true. Your boss is under pressure because corporate says your local shop must produce a certain number of widgets per hour in order to be profitable. You think a widget should be "just so" and consistently produce fewer but better pieces per hour. Do not be surprised when you get passed over for promotion or worse, released from your job. The "loyal" employee is the one who puts his shoulder against the plow and uses his hard work and creativity to help get the overall widget count up. "He's just sucking up to the boss!" No, he's working toward the same goal. He's loyal to the mission.

Most of the leaders surveyed had zero tolerance toward those who had different goals than the company. One actually said, "If you want your own vision, start your own company!" Another said, "A person who is loyal "gets" the vision in that he understands that the firm is working towards *something*, understands that he has a part that he is responsible for in order for the firm to reach that *something*, and aligns his goals with the firm's so that his successes support the firm's and visa versa." The point is that your job is one part that relates to the whole. If you don't understand the big picture, you don't really understand your job. Worse, if you work to you own end, you may actually be working against the purpose of your boss and the organization he/she leads!

When you catch the vision – understand the mission of the company – it enables you to see your job in a brand new light. It gives reason to the mundane, purpose to the routine, and perspective for the "arbitrary." To make this point, one leader related the story of the three masons. A man on the street approached a man laying bricks. The brick layer was slow but deliberate, showing little emotion. He did a good job; put in his eight hours, and went home after collecting his check. The man on the street asked, "What are you doing?" The brick layer replied, "I am laying bricks."

A little farther down the road the man on the street saw a man working on the same project. This mason was happy enough to do his job and put forth an effort to make sure the lines were straight and the mortar smooth. It seemed his work brought him some pleasure. "What are you doing," asked the man on the street? "I am building a wall," the brick layer replied.

Finally, the man on the street approached a third mason who whistled while he worked. His joy was obvious and he took great pride in his task. He worked like a fine craftsman, each brick was important. He made hard work seem effortless. Once again the man on the street asked, "What are you doing?" With a smile and a sense of satisfaction, the third brick layer replied, "I am building a cathedral!"

Each man worked on the same job for the same company. Each man had the same mission. One man saw only bricks, the other only the wall but the third saw the finished product. He saw the vision. In seeing it, he owned it. In owning it, he worked for it. In working for it, he demonstrated loyalty. If you owned the company which one would you promote?

I stumbled into this principle quite by accident when I worked my way through Bible college. I worked for a shipping company that was growing at a very rapid rate. The package volume handled by our center was continually on the increase. My job at the time was loading package cars. We worked from 3:30 AM until 7:30AM each morning and were paid quite handsomely. For our pay, they expected us to work at a break-neck pace. We HAD to be completely done by 8:00 AM or the company would lose money by the minute. Most of the guys on the line didn't care. More time on the clock meant more money in our paycheck.

The bottle-neck was always the "unload." This was where the tractor trailer trucks were unloaded onto a belt. Once these packages hit the belt they were flipped (labels up) and sorted. They then rode down a belt where loaders loaded package cars. That belt moved so fast that it was almost impossible to keep up. If a loader got behind ("blown away") packages would fall all over the floor, unharmed, but impeding the loader's ability to move quickly. It was a hassle to get blown away. Loaders preferred a nice smooth easy sort – easy work, big money. In order for the company to make money on the morning pre-load, loaders were going to have to get blown away.

I don't know when the idea hit me. No one suggested it. It just came to me. My father always told me that the best job security was "a job well done". So, everyday, somewhere in the middle of the morning sort when I was all caught up, I would jump off the line and run into the back where the tractor trailers were being unloaded. I would jump into one of the trucks and start unloading beside the other three guys back there with all I had. I wasn't a big guy. In fact, I was one of the smallest and youngest employees. (To look at me you would never think, "hire him" much less, "promote him.") After ten minutes of this, the volume on the belt swelled so that multiple loaders were being blown away. They would shut off the belt to slow things down, angry and frustrated. The supervisors, elated at the increased volume would cut the belt back on to keep things moving. The sort was shortened. The trucks were loaded on time. The company made money.

When I returned to my section of cars, I was blown away beyond belief. I hustled for the rest of the morning sort to get my cars loaded and clocked out on schedule. I never told my bosses what I was doing. One day as I returned to my section a supervisor happened by and saw the terrible mess. He rebuked me, "What have you been doing, man! Clean up this mess!" I informed him that I had been in the unload. He stared at me and asked incredulously, "That was you? Is that you everyday?"

I didn't work for the paycheck; I worked for the company. Their goal was to make money (or at least not lose it) during the morning sort. To do my job right I had to adopt that as my goal as well. The company looked at me as a loyal employee. Why? I saw their vision and aligned my job with that goal.

About a month later, that same supervisor asked me (one of the smallest and youngest employees) if I would like to be promoted into supervision. I took the job and became the boss of all the "paycheck guys." Thanks, Dad, the best job security is a job well done. Well done means you demonstrate loyalty by being committed to the vision.

Chapter Three Reflection Questions:

1. What is the mission or vision of the company, unit, or institution you work for?
2. How does your job relate to that vision?
3. Are you perceived as loyal? Does your boss think you "own" the vision? How do you know?
4. What new actions can you initiate on your job, beginning right now, that will communicate your commitment to the mission?

Chapter Four

Integrity

Being able to Engender Trust from Your
Employer and Co-workers

Psalm 15:1-4 (NKJV) *"Lord, who may abide in Your tabernacle? Who may dwell on Your holy hill? He who walks uprightly, and works righteousness, and speaks truth in his heart; He does not backbite with his tongue, nor does evil to his neighbor, nor does he take up a reproach against a friend; in whose eyes a vile person is despised, but he honors those who fear the Lord; he who swears to his own hurt and does not change."*

"To really get ahead in this world you have to be smart!" I wonder how many fathers have passed on that falsehood as good advice over the years. I am not against intelligence or education – far from it. I simply no longer believe that brains and knowledge are the top commodities for advancement. They say in the worlds of business and economics that cash is king. Well, in the job market, character, not intelligence, is king. Employers are looking for more than people with smarts; they are looking for people they can trust! This is truer today than ever. Scandal after scandal has only proven that business without integrity; no, *life* without integrity leads to disaster and great loss.

"You can trust me!" That is not the point. The real question is, can you engender trust from your boss and co-workers? Can you live in such a way as to *cause* them to trust you? It doesn't really matter what you think of yourself; what counts here is the appraisal your boss, co-workers, and clients make of you. What you think about yourself determines how you live and how you feel about your life. What they (boss, co-workers, and clients) think about you dictates how they live toward you which, in large part, determines your future!

On one level, integrity is demonstrated everyday. It has to do with how you do your job and how you routinely conduct yourself around your employer, co-workers, and clients. One successful business leader put it this way, "Integrity means being consistent – doing what you say you're going to do and then doing all that needs to be done in order to do it." To punctuate his point he said of himself, "You can expect from me what I tell you I'm going to do!" In the old days, a man's word was all you needed "because a man is only as good as his word." Business deals could be consummated on a handshake. While the legal nature of things has demanded that hard copy contracts replace handshakes, it seems that a man is still only as good as his word. If a man doesn't keep his word routinely, he isn't considered a good man! He may work hard and "have a good heart," but in the world of work, he is considered a bruised reed. You can't lean on him; he'll let you down.

Ask yourself the tough questions – are you a person of your word? Do you do what you say you are going to do? Do you really have integrity or do you just say that you do?

We all know people who make commitments and then later cancel. We understand that happening in the case of emergencies or when life "throws a curve-ball." But many people cancel according to convenience as personal comfort dictates. "Sorry, we can't make it after all." And yet, you planned with these people in mind. The truth is, they valued their own personal comfort over their word, and you ended up the injured party. They lacked integrity. Confront them with that fact and you know you'll have a fight on your hands. So, you say nothing. But your trust in them withers.

The Bible text listed at the beginning of the chapter uses the phrase, "swear to your own hurt." That simply means, once you give your word, you fulfill it – even if it hurts. It means you come through even if it costs you time or money, or if it is inconvenient, or if you are tired, or if you'd rather do something else, or if a great opportunity opens up. You just do what you said you were going to do. People who live like that have integrity. The others don't – period. They may claim to, but as the old saying goes, "actions speak louder than words."

People who live like this in their personal lives, live like this at work. Employers are looking for people they can trust – people with integrity. Integrity means being able to engender trust from your employer and co-workers. When a new position opens, the employee trusted by the boss easily gets the job. When a client decides to buy, the agent who engenders trust gets the sale. When a reference is needed, the employee who is trusted gets the stellar recommendation, on-and-on it goes. In the job market, character is king, and the king of character is integrity.

You can "take this to the bank" – someone is always watching. You may never know it is happening, but people watch what you do and how you respond to what life throws at you. The majority of the time, you do not get the chance to explain your actions. Integrity is more than just keeping your word. One leader said, "Integrity is the hidden man – who you are when no one is watching." But the truth is, someone is always watching, and often, we are unaware.

We all can think of a myriad of circumstances where we found ourselves in a position to observe someone who had no idea they were under observation. I remember a time I was considering a number of people for promotion into a position of leadership. During that process, while driving through town, I observed one of the men in consideration furiously chewing out his wife. I chose another candidate.

Some friends, co-workers, and I attended a ministers' conference in another state. Upon checking out of the hotel, one of my friends stood in line behind one of the speakers. As the speaker closed out his account he asked to "pay for the movie in cash." Reflecting on the speaker's controversial stance concerning his acceptance of post-modern society's rejection of absolutes, my friend wondered why he wanted to pay cash. Why wouldn't he want a record of the movie he watched? Who knows, it could have been a Disney movie. Given the circumstances, what do you think? Integrity has to do with the hidden man, but nothing is really hidden. Someone is always watching.

Playing computer games on company time, taking a few extra minutes for a personal break while on an errand for the boss, padding the expense account, fudging on your mileage, taking home office supplies, making personal use of the company postage meter, coming in late but having a friend clock you in, calling in sick to take a personal day, undermining another employee in the office to make yourself look good, slacking off when the boss is out are ways, along with many others, that people demonstrate a lack of integrity. Many employers would consider most of the items in the list above stealing. "Oh, come on, you are over-reacting!" Am I? Consider the following.

"Trust – this is a deal breaker! I can train somebody I can trust. I WILL NOT train somebody I cannot trust. I will not waste his time or mine." Now those are strong words and the sentiment captured in them was echoed over and over by the leaders I surveyed. Integrity is not defined in terms of your evaluation of yourself. Integrity has to do with the evaluation made about you by those around you. The issue at hand, therefore, is this – it all falls back on your ability to engender trust from your employer, co-workers, friends, and clients.

Section Three of this book deals with the "Five Fatal Blunders: What Not to Do if You Want to Get Ahead" but I must bring up one issue related to integrity. Leaders were so strong on this issue of trust, that one entrepreneur and business owner flatly stated, "#1 Fatal Blunder? Lying! Enough said!" Those with integrity today are at a premium and employers are looking for them. Simply put, they will get ahead in life. Those without integrity may temporarily move on but eventually it will catch up to them. They float along in life, feeling misunderstood. Those who violate the principle of integrity get fired. It seems that, after faithfulness, the ability to engender trust from your employer, co-workers, and clients might just be the most important of these seven traits. Do you possess it? How do you know? Everybody claims to have integrity, but unfortunately, few really do. Are you in that number?

Chapter Four Reflection Questions:

1. Do you agree with the author's functional definition of integrity? Why or why not?

2. Do you routinely make promises or commitments and fail to follow through or go back on your word? Ask three people to help you answer that question.

   A. A friend or spouse

   B. A trusted co-worker

   C. Your employer (Suggestion: Make an appointment to see your boss. Tell her that you are working on your lifestyle to increase your "promotability" as an employee. Explain to her the definition of integrity – being able to engender trust from your employer and co-workers. Ask her if you possess this character quality and for suggestions on improvement. This meeting alone will begin to build a bond of trust, especially if you follow through on her suggestions!)

3. Think of times when you have broken your word to others. Purpose to go back to apologize and to make amends.

Chapter Five

Diligence
Being willing to Take Initiative

Proverbs 10:4 (NKJV) "He who has a slack hand becomes poor, but the hand of the diligent makes rich."

Proverbs 12:24 (NKJV) "The hand of the diligent will rule, but the lazy man will be put to forced labor."

"Good help is so hard to find these days! People just don't work like they used to." That sentiment enjoys the status of "Universal Consensus" among employers. I have heard that statement, or its equivalent, from employers *many* times in recent years. But I also remember being a small boy and hearing that same thing from my elders. It seems that "good help" has always been hard to come by.

The "good help is hard to find" proposition is normally followed by complaints like; "can't turn your back on them – they'll quit working;" or "have to tell them every little thing;" or "they can't think for themselves;" and the list goes on. At every level and in every company or institution, work must be done and workers must be hired to do it. A great deal of time and effort is spent on the part of employers in finding workers who will do that work in a way and at a rate that reflects their values and satisfies their goals. "Good workers" are at a premium in the workforce today.

Most mid to large-sized companies spend huge amounts of money on departments whose sole purpose is to find, train, and keep good workers. These departments have nothing to do with creating new products (research and development), selling the products they produce, or insuring the quality of their present line. They focus only on finding, training, and keeping good workers. Yes, a stream of good workers is worth millions. From the small mom-and-pop shop to the Fortune 500 conglomerate the most precious commodity on the market is human – the "good worker."

One thing is for certain, a hard working person will always have a job. And in the workplace, all things being equal, the hard worker is usually first in line for promotion. But everyone fancies themselves a good or hard worker. They look down the hall or across the assembly line and measure themselves by someone who puts in less effort for the same money – the slacker. "I deserve more. I work much harder for the same pay." Could it be that employers measure differently? What do they think of when they use the term "good" or "hard" worker?

A word often used along with these two terms is the word "diligence." It seems an easy term to understand at first glance. "It means hard worker." But a closer examination reveals much more.

The word in the Hebrew language, as quoted in the two verses above, means "to rise early to a task." This eliminates the idea of being late or of perpetually working behind. The diligent person doesn't do that. This person approaches work before work begins. They "rise early" or are prepared before work begins. The implications are manifold.

First, preparation requires an understanding of the job. How can one "rise early to a task" unless they understand exactly what that task is. You may know "what" your job is but do you know the "why" that lies behind it? Most workers focus on the "what" – the tasks outlined in the job description, or how many widgets he is supposed to produce, or how many policies she is supposed to sell. Most employers focus on the "why" of a specific job. Why was this job description created? Why did the company choose that specific number of widgets? Why was the sales goal for this quarter set at this number of insurance policies? People who come to work understanding the "why" behind a job work with an edge, a slice of motivation and dedication other workers don't share. We have all heard a musician who just plays the notes written on the page. The music is all there but the player plays from the head. Then there is the musician who really understands the piece. She flows with the music and plays from the heart. These musicians capture us and draw us in. They more than read the notes they understand the music and bring it to life as they play. Diligent workers don't just play the notes and go through the motions. They bring work to life because they understand their job.

Second, diligent workers understand how their job fits into the company's goals. Being a cashier, for instance, is more than just taking money from a customer. It is the first stage of money management. Accurate accounting begins with an accurate count. Also, in many companies, the cash register is a key "cog" in the whole inventory process. What happens at checkout greatly impacts which products are reordered in what quantity, and which products get dropped. Finally, the cashier is often the last face of customer service. What happens in that line can "seal the deal" on not just making the sale but whether or not that customer will shop someplace else on their next shopping trip or become a customer for life! What are your company's goals, both long and short term? How does your job relate to those goals? If you don't know, ask. Don't be embarrassed. Your boss will not be put off by the question. On the contrary, it is her dream to have employees who care enough about the company to ask such questions. (Employers would be well served in communicating these types of things to employees on a regular basis. A well informed employee is a well armed employee and more easily motivated.)

Third, diligence implies a willingness on the part of the worker to do all it takes to "make it happen" on the job. Remember this – a job description, no matter how complete it seems, is only an introduction to the job. Every job includes implied tasks too numerous and too varied to innumerate. Employees who recognize this and do what it takes to isolate those implied tasks and perform them differentiate themselves from the crowd and set themselves up for promotion. One business leader said, "A good worker does not have to be 'the sharpest tool in the shed,' but if they work without wavering, that person will be considered very valuable and will be rewarded." This requires some thought and preparation – "rising early to the task."

In short, being diligent demands a willingness on the part of the employee to take initiative. Stating the proposition in the negative, one female entrepreneur said diligence means, "not waiting to be told what to do next." Another put it this way, a person with initiative "actively pursues additional responsibility. He doesn't remain idle when projects are complete. Instead, he let's you know he wants more to do and actively pursues the next thing." One might respond, "If I ask for more to do, my boss might give me more without giving me more pay!" I guess you are working for the check! Forgive me, but that is so short sighted and selfish. Selfish because the company didn't hire you to collect a check; they hired you to do a job, complete with its implied tasks. Short-sighted because you are ignoring the pathway to increased prosperity that goes with promotion for fear of missing out on a few dollars!

Your boss knows who is working for the check and who is working for the company. You can't fake it. Those who work for a check do the minimum. Those who work for the company demonstrate diligence by taking initiative. I quote again from the survey: a person with initiative "consistently performs above the standard. They are not willing to compromise, know what is expected, and strive to surpass the standard whenever possible."

In the words of famed chef, Emeril Lagasse, let's "take it up a notch." Consider the words of Paul in Colossians 3:23, 24 (NIV), "Whatever you do, work at it with all your heart, as working for the Lord, not for men, since you know that you will receive an inheritance from the Lord as a reward. It is the Lord Christ you are serving." Paul upgrades my advice to work for the company rather than just work for the check; he admonishes us to work directly for Christ. This is genius! Maybe your boss is hard to work for. Maybe the conditions you find yourself working in are almost intolerable. The Christian has a higher motivation. He works for God in the midst of a human environment. He comes to work thinking that he will work as if God owns the company, as if God is his boss, as if God is watching both his actions and his heart. He comes to work with a faith that promotion comes from the Lord and that God will reward him for his labor. He realizes that God is bigger than the boss and actually holds the heart of the boss in His hand (Proverbs 21:1). Because of that, the Lord can turn the heart of the boss any way He wants to. He can grant favor to the employee in the eyes of the employer. He can, and according to the verse, will reward the employee for his service to Him. Working for Christ is a higher motivation than simply working for a human organization and releases a whole new level of passion and creativity. Leaders in the workplace see this motivation and passion and interpret it as zeal for the institution and its goals. Workers with passion and zeal demonstrate that they are diligent by displaying initiative and differentiate themselves from the pack. They put themselves in line for promotion. Once promoted, they take their new elevated status as a reward from God which only heightens their sense of commitment. It is a never ending upward spiral. Genius! God really knows what He is doing!

Do you want to get promoted? There really is no middle ground. The verses at the beginning of this chapter draw very clear lines. The "slack hand" (tough words) becomes poor. They get stuck in the workforce at the same level while the cost of living rises. "The hand of the diligent makes rich." She is on the upward spiral of increase. In similar fashion, "the hand of the diligent will rule." At the end of the day, it is the diligent worker, the one willing to take initiative who gets promoted. She steps to the next level. But "the lazy man (tough words again) will be put to forced labor." They are under supervision and have to be watched and continually told what to do next, since they do not automatically reach for the next task. Since they are not diligent, since they do not take initiative, they will end up feeling as if they are engaged in slave labor with a boss or master always looking over their shoulder. Which life would you like to live? In the end, there are two types of workers, those who take initiative and those who do not, those who get promoted and those who do not.

Chapter Five Reflection Questions:

1. What are the implied tasks related to your job?

2. What unspoken expectations might your boss have of you in conjunction with those implied tasks?

3. Honestly ask yourself, "Do I work for the check, the company, or for the Lord?" How do you communicate that on your job?

4. List three things you can do to demonstrate diligence and take initiative on your job.

Chapter Six

Team Player
Being Committed to Another's Success as Well as Your Own

Phil 2:3, 4 (NIV) "Do nothing out of selfish ambition or vain conceit, but in humility consider others better than yourselves. Each of you should look not only to your own interests, but also to the interests of others."

In a "dog-eat-dog" world where everyone is trying to get ahead, and like a pyramid, the number of opportunities for advancement become narrower toward the top, this point seems counter-intuitive. Why would someone want to help their peers get ahead and risk being overlooked for a promotion themselves? Be careful! Do not miss this point! Selfishness is a clear sign that a person works only for his own benefit – not an endearing trait to employers. But a team player – one who is committed to others' successes as well as his own – reveals a set of motives fondly embraced by leaders in the workplace.

Michael Jordan is undoubtedly the best basketball player who ever lived. He is a legend. But in his early days with the Chicago Bulls, he couldn't "buy" a championship. Still, Michael was a thrill to watch; any game could suddenly turn into an instant highlight film. And Michael was a scoring machine. The numbers he put up every night were astounding. He was also an outstanding defensive player – again, the best player who ever lived, still no championship! Enter Coach Phil Jackson. Jackson, after studying the team stats, noted that the team was more likely to lose when Michael scored more than 30 points a game, but their win-loss record was far better when he averaged under the 30-point mark. Remarkable! Basketball is a team sport and Michael's lower but substantial point contribution meant that the team had to put forth an increased effort to win games. Michael would draw the defense when he touched the ball. But then, he would distribute it to the open player for the easier basket. Michael's lower point total meant that all the other players had to "step up" their game. That's what happens when we play "team ball" – we make the other players around us better.

As it turns out, business is a team sport as well. The most successful companies know this quite well. The world's top companies work very hard to create a "family" atmosphere that under girds the "corporate culture" they spend millions trying to impart to their employees. All of this is designed to convert the "I" to the "we" of business. They want employees to adopt a style or culture of business that will connect them to the company's values and with all the other employees who they hope share those values. While every company wants to hire great workers, those at the top know that the "superstar" may not, in the end, make the company better. One business owner said, "You're looking for the right person not necessarily the best person – not the superstar." Who is the right person? In addition to being the right person to fit a certain job, employers hope for a bonus. They hope, in the hiring process, to stumble on a few team players – those who galvanize the workforce and make other employees in the shop better.

In the workplace, true "team play" is every employer's dream. Owners and managers drool over the idea of a group of employees who will work as a team to accomplish company goals. Most never see it. The people who work for them, work only for themselves – for the check. Occasionally, some kind soul chips in during a tough time to help some fellow worker accomplish a task. But as a lifestyle – seldom seen! Often the most prized human asset in an organization is the one who can get others to work together. That type of employee is almost never found on the "floor" because they have been quickly moved up into management. This type of catalyst is a truly rare and precious commodity. These people are almost guaranteed to get ahead. Are you that type of employee? What does a team player look like?

A team player, "Shows concern for others. He/she is an empathetic co-worker." You can't be self-absorbed and be a team player. You cannot be unaware of the human landscape around you and be a team player. The people who serve as catalysts for cooperation in the workplace are people who are connected to other people. They have listened to the hurts, needs, and view points of others, and in doing so, they have earned the right to be heard. In every culture, on every continent, in every factory, school yard, or place of employment, the people who care, count. People are prone to trust those who they feel care about them. That place of trust is the incubator of lots of good stuff to include team work. The motives of a caring person almost never come into question and folks are more likely to pitch in to accomplish a common goal when they feel they are in an environment free of manipulation and ambition. An employee can often pull this off better than the boss. Workers know that it is the boss's job to motivate them to work, but when the inspiration to pitch in comes from a trusted, caring friend in the workplace, the natural resistance to serve others is low. Yes, team players are a rare and precious commodity indeed!

The same business leader I quoted above added this to the list of qualities that describe such a catalyst. She said a team player, "remains attuned to office politics but does not participate in gossip." This quality describes the difference between one who is gathering the workforce around a task and one who is stealing hearts in order to produce a rebellion. True team players connect with people but they work for the company. In the end, they are committed to the team and strongly desire its success. Consequently, this type of employee is aware of discontent but refuses to be drawn in by it. What kind of person is this? A person who has buried his own selfish ambition, as described in the verses at the beginning of this chapter. This is a person who is against everything that is against the team. Office gossip, discontent, negative and complaining attitudes can destroy team play. A team cannot exist; it cannot win, in such an environment. Employers are almost never included in the circles where these types of things are freely shared. Team players are their best assets in such places and at such times. They are invaluable. Once an employer spots you in the role of team builder, you will never lack for opportunities for advancement.

Notice that the Scripture verses also mention that "each of you should look not only to your own interests, but also to the interests of others." It doesn't say you should not look out for your own interests. It just says you should not look *exclusively* to your own interests. In looking out for what is good for you, look out also for what is good for others. In fact, the truly smart employee knows that, in the long run, his own interests are best served by the success of the company. And the company's success is determined by the workforce employed by that organization. Therefore, he/she guarantees his/her own future by helping others succeed. In my notes from a seminar on leadership and success, I quoted John Maxwell as saying, "Success is about sowing seeds that benefit others because success is not just about you." Employers recognize that for an organization to be successful it will require a team effort. Team players will always have a job and never lack opportunity for advancement!

The thirty-one leaders I interviewed shared a common disdain for those in their employ who "do their own thing" – the opposite of team play. This person, in the eyes of the boss, is using the job and the institution to accomplish his/her own goals. Philippians 2:3 (NIV) calls this "selfish ambition." One entrepreneur said, "I have no problem with failure, but I will not tolerate someone with their own agenda!"

What kind of employee are you? I did not ask what kind of employee do you want to be. Nor did I ask what type of employee do you think you are. What kind of employee are you? Are you caring and empathetic? Are you committed to harmony in the workplace or are office problems "somebody else's problem?" Are you committed to creating a cooperative environment? Are the company's goals your goals or do you work for goals of your own?

Chapter Six Reflection Questions:

1. Think of a person from your past who others would consider a team player. What characteristics of team play were exemplified in his/her life? List them. Do you possess these?

2. In your workplace, what would it take to create an environment of cooperation? Of those needs, which ones are in the realm of your control – stuff you could do something about? Turn those needs into actions. Prioritize them. Begin with the top three and attempt to implement them immediately.

3. List the names of the people with whom you work directly. What are their needs? Desires? Dreams? Life goals? What can you do to better connect with these people?

Chapter Seven

Emotional Intelligence
Being Able to Relate Well With Others

1 Chronicles 12:32 (NKJV) "of the sons of Issachar who had understanding of the times, to know what Israel ought to do."

Proverbs 2:9-11 (NIV) "Then you will understand what is right and just and fair – every good path. For wisdom will enter your heart, and knowledge will be pleasant to your soul. Discretion will protect you, and understanding will guard you."

One of the business leaders I surveyed handed me an article he had taken from an airline in-flight magazine he read on a recent business trip. It was an interview of a man named Richard Boyatzis, Ph.D. who had co-authored a book entitled <u>Resonant Leadership</u>. The title of the article was "How Great Leaders Lead," and carried the subtitle "Forget book or street smarts; its emotional intelligence that matters most." I have a couple of books on my shelf that deal with the concept of emotional intelligence, so I was familiar with the term and the thought related to it. But let me say, while the term, "emotional intelligence," may be new, the truth behind it is as old as mankind. Solomon, the author of most of the Book of Proverbs in the Bible, captured the concept and condensed its finer points into couplets in chapter after chapter all throughout the book. The point is people who know people, can anticipate how people will respond and how situations are likely to turnout are the ones who get ahead in life. Most of the others watch, and some simply don't have a clue!

The definition of emotional intelligence I will use here is entirely my own and one designed to fit the discussion of this book – how to get ahead in life. Simply put, emotional intelligence is defined in terms of how we handle ourselves and our relationships. It includes an awareness of where people are emotionally and mentally *in the moment* and the ability to understand how to relate to them and potentially move them to a desired action.

- How to handle an angry customer or a disgruntled employee
- How to get a point across to a potential client who is emotionally detached from the product
- How to quiet a pushy person
- How to bring peace between two warring individuals in the office
- How to correct an employee and have them walk away thanking you for it
- How to anticipate a negative response and create an answer before the negative response is given

These are just a few examples of a place where a person with emotional intelligence shines. We have all been around a person who, not properly appraising where a person is emotionally, pushes a situation one step too far causing himself and the customer or employee both embarrassment and further upset. In contrast, we have also seen the person in similar circumstances who refuses to handle the situation at all who simply "rolls over" and lets the disgruntled person have their way. In both cases, the person involved in dealing with a situation lacked emotional intelligence.

We have seen people say something or handle a situation in such a way that brought them personal satisfaction but caused them to lose credibility with the crowd. "I took care of that!" Yes, but people no longer respect you like they did! We have seen people use the "I'll just run you over" approach to getting things done. But in the end, people don't love those who intimidate them. And yet, intimidators either do not recognize that or do not care. Either way, they lack emotional intelligence. Those who simply avoid conflict prove before they start that they lack emotional intelligence. Their passivity admits that they do not know how to handle the situation. The interesting thing is that most people who have a high emotional IQ do not know what they will do when they enter into a difficult situation either. They simply walk into it, observing, listening, evaluating, sizing up the people and the level of potential hostility and look for an opportunity to take control of the climate, so they can turn it and the people involved in a positive direction. One thing is for certain, people who regularly offend others or who are easily offended themselves *do not* have good people skills. These people often blame others for the relational upset in their lives and never seem to recognize that the common thread of the conflict they have faced over the years leads back to them.

Organizations spend thousands of dollars training people how to deal with conflict, how to know when to close a deal, how to handle customer complaints, or how to motivate employees. The list goes on. These are good things, but do you know why they send employees to these training seminars? Because, a formal education, street smarts, and years of experience are no substitute for emotional intelligence. While people may come to work trained *for* work, they do not necessarily possess the skills to deal with the people *at* work! So, we teach them what to do in specific situations, how to handle a certain set of circumstances. Learning information alone will not raise a person's emotional IQ. And yet, the business world is coming to realize that the most important parts of success do not necessarily come from education or life experience, as important as they may be. People skills are a prerequisite for success. People are not static. They do not come in boxes and the circumstances that surround their lives do not come in prepackaged sitcom situations that automatically resolve themselves in thirty minutes minus commercials. To be successful, we must deal with people and the stuff of their lives as they are presented to us on a daily basis. To deal with people we must possess people skills or emotional intelligence.

Employers agree. The terms they use may differ but there is almost universal agreement that people skills trump pure knowledge alone. (This should come as good news for those of us in the workforce who are of average natural intelligence.) One leader commented, "You must know people, understand each of their situations, treat them with dignity and respect, and have a genuine interest in them." Fellow employees are people. Customers are people. The competition is comprised of people. Suppliers and distributors are people. Bosses are people. Without an ability to navigate skillfully through the maze of human interaction, a person desiring to get promoted, to get ahead in life, is completely lost. People with people skills "communicate effectively up and down the chain of command. They are assertive without being offensive. They are able to handle a crisis with finesse always striving to find a win-win solution when possible," said one of the surveyed bosses. These people, as described by the leaders in my survey are the ones who get ahead. It is almost automatic! Employees must find a way to increase their emotional intelligence!

Is it possible for someone to raise his/her emotional IQ? Some people are natural athletes. Some possess the ability to run faster than others with minimal to no training. Others are naturally strong, their build and metabolism set them up to put on muscle in response to targeted exercise. Those without the right natural composition can lift all they like and they will never obtain the perfect build. They just don't have the body for it. The same it true in the realm of the intellect. There are those who are born with IQ's above the rest. They learn without trying. Others study and cram but still never match the test scores of the intellectual elite. The same holds true in so many other areas of life – singing, creating art, writing, public speaking, selling, leading, and the list goes on. Does that list also include emotional intelligence? Are there those who naturally possess a level of people skills to which few others will be able to attain? Are there those who were born with the natural potential to understand people and comprehend the possible outcomes of circumstances without training? Yes, some people have a naturally high emotional IQ.

They are often hard to detect in the early years of life. You can't test for emotional IQ on standard achievement tests or in a high school social studies class. You can't detect the presence of these people by surveying the role of academic achievers. People with naturally high emotional IQ's are just as likely to be found at the bottom of the academic "food chain" as they are at the top. They are bright but not bright in a way that shows up on traditional academic measuring tools. Think back to the list of people who were given awards at your high school superlatives' ceremony. Many times, "Most likely to Succeed" doesn't, at least not in the way he/she was expected to. And there are always a few in the graduating class who people never would have picked to succeed who do really well. Looking back, the majority of the ones who did well possessed some measure of emotional intelligence. Whether they did well academically or not, they had that certain knack for understanding their situation and how to navigate through to come out smelling like a rose. The kid who talked his way into trouble but always managed to talk his way out, probably went on to talk himself into a job and then talk his way through, over the years, to regional manager. These people are like the athletes who are naturally fast or the student who is naturally smart – it is part of their make-up. But for the rest of us there is good news.

I used to think that we were stuck in our situation with little we could do to change. The person with the average IQ cannot make himself smarter. The person with average speed will never make the US Olympic team. But upon further reflection, I realized I was wrong. I should have known better. Personally, I am not a natural athlete, but I have had the privilege of competing and doing well in a number of sporting endeavors over the years. I am not naturally bright, but I graduated Bible College with a 3.93 GPA. In both cases, I worked very hard to get there, but I got there. We all have our limitations, but with some focused effort we can improve in areas where learning is possible. Can we raise our level of emotional intelligence? Yes!

How does someone raise their emotional IQ? There are the obvious answers like, take a class, or find a mentor with a high EIQ (emotional IQ), but who teaches a class on such a thing? Besides, EIQ is not an academic discipline. It is true that some things are better "caught than taught" and emotional intelligence certainly fits into that category, but who can find a mentor who has the time to coach us through all the subtle nuances of the choices we make in how we relate to the people around us and the circumstances they create? There is another way. Turn to Solomon! PROVERBS @ DAY

As I said before, Solomon, King of Israel, wrote most of the proverbs – gems of emotional intelligence – in the book of Proverbs. Solomon was known for his wisdom. Scripture never says he was smart but it does say he was wise. The historical narrative of his life as recorded in the Bible bears that out. Even the Queen of Sheba came seeking an audience with him to see if the rumors about him were true. She left amazed. In the second chapter, Solomon talks about the benefits one might expect to receive from an earnest, life-long search for wisdom. The whole book is based on the idea that wisdom is obtainable; it can be gained. It may be added to one's life. At this point you may be saying, "I need emotional intelligence, not wisdom." Perhaps some functional definitions of wisdom are in order. Wisdom is knowing how to live successfully. (And isn't life all about relationships – people skills?) Wisdom is knowing what principle to apply when, depending on the situation. Wisdom is knowing how to relate to people in the varying circumstances of life. Wisdom contains emotional intelligence. Those with wisdom have high emotional IQs.

Some of the benefits listed in the second chapter of Proverbs are included in the verses quoted at the beginning of this chapter. Proverbs 2:9-11 (NIV) "Then you will understand what is right and just and fair – every good path. For wisdom will enter your heart, and knowledge will be pleasant to your soul. Discretion will protect you, and understanding will guard you." Let me break it down for you:

1. "understand what is right and fair – every good path" – This is the way things ought to be done. When someone suggests such a solution (right and fair – the good path) to a problem, reasonable people resonate with the suggestion. While others are still searching for the appropriate action, Solomon says that the person who seeks wisdom will know what to do.

2. "wisdom will enter your heart" – As you read the book of Proverbs you find that the first step of wisdom is to seek wisdom. It seems that all true seekers find, and that the act of seeking is wisdom itself! Here, we find a clear promise that we can grow in this area. We may not be able to run much faster or sing much better, but we can add wisdom and increase our EIQ! Wisdom is the answer to the question

"how." How does this work? How do we solve this problem? How do we proceed from here?

3. "knowledge will be pleasant to your soul" – This is not simply general knowledge. This is the knowledge of how life works. Knowledge is the answer to the question "what." What is going on here? What is the problem? A search for wisdom yields the product of creating a thirst for more "people knowledge," a thirst that is always satisfied.

4. "discretion will protect you" – Discretion is the ability to quickly decide between a right and wrong course of action. What a valuable tool that is! Solomon says that seeking wisdom will cause a person to operate at increased levels of discretion, thus protecting them for making mistakes in dealing with life circumstances.

5. "understanding will guard you" – Understanding is the answer to the question "why." It is the knowledge of the underlying causes of a thing. Why is this happening? Why does this work this way? Why does she react to me?

All of the above are central elements of emotional intelligence. The book is "chalked-full" of truth statements designed to make one wiser. I suggest you *slowly* read the chapter of Proverbs that corresponds to each day of the month – on the 10th read chapter 10, on the 28th read chapter 28. Let the verses read you as much or more than you read them. If you seek His way of dealing with things, He promises to make sure you get the knowledge, understanding, discretion, and wisdom you need to operate at the highest and best level possible in your present situation. A little effort and you can elevate your EIQ!

Chapter Seven Reflection Questions:

1. Think of someone you would say has emotional intelligence. What characteristics stand out that give you that impression? Which ones can you emulate?

2. In what ways do you lack emotional intelligence? List the gaps, the areas where you feel you are lacking.

3. How do you plan to acquire increased EI in those areas?

4. Ask someone to evaluate your personal levels of EI.

5. Write your own personal definition of emotional intelligence. If you fulfill that definition, will you achieve your goal of increasing your emotional IQ?

EIQ: CHARACTERISTICS

JOE MOORE   LISTENS & HIS HEART; ASKS PROBING Q'S

DARLA CASNER ANSWERS DIRECTLY & CONVICTION; THEN GOES AWAY praying

PAT KAPUSNIK SHE SEEMS TO JOIN YOUR SIDE OF SITUATION AND FEEL WHAT YOU FEEL EVEN IF SHE HAS NO QUICK ANSWERS AND CAN'T EVEN UNDERSTAND

DICK BIGELLO   TENDS TO HAVE A READY ANSWER, BUT YOU FEEL LIKE HE PRAYS LATER.

MERRIE BIGELLO SHE CAN SEE ALL ELEMENTS OF A SITUATION, AND IS NOT SQUEMISH ABOUT SAYING WHAT NEEDS TO BE DONE, EVEN TO YOUR FACE, EVEN IF IT IS A HARD ANSWER.

Chapter Eight

Teachable
Being willing to Learn New Things and Accept Instruction

Matthew 5:5 (NKJV) "Blessed are the meek, for they shall inherit the earth."

Reading this you might think, "I don't need the whole earth, I just want to get ahead. I just want a promotion!" This verse comes from the Sermon on the Mount, one of Jesus' messages that is among the most often quoted and most beloved passages of Scripture. The truths shared here have enjoyed almost universal acceptance in nearly every culture throughout the ages. And the promise holds true; special benefits await those who are meek. Note that the benefits of meekness are not reserved for heaven. In fact no mention of heaven is made in the verse at all. Jesus is saying the opposite here; those who are meek reap the reward on earth, in this lifetime. There is an inheritance reserved for those who possess this trait. But what exactly is this trait?

Many hear "meek" and think "weak." They conjure up an image if a person too afraid to speak or stand up for himself, a person who perpetually gets the "raw end of the deal" and has learned to live with it. The words "mild mannered" and "meek," in the minds of many, go hand-in-hand. And yet the Biblical idea behind the word is a word picture of a work animal in a harness. The picture is one of power under control – a strong animal, a horse or an ox perhaps who is able to be guided wherever the master desires. The animal is broken and tamed yet powerful, able to take instruction, and willing to use his power to accomplish a goal determined by another. As you can see, the meaning Jesus had in mind is quite the opposite of "weak." Perhaps the best word in the English language that fits the concept is "teachable."

We have already seen that leaders today are not looking for knowledge or ability but character, as in the qualities I have already mentioned in subsequent chapters. (This next sentence is key!) Leaders feel they are able to teach and train an employee what he needs to know as long as that employee is teachable. More and more businesses are creating their own corporate culture, even small businesses. Led by the example of giant conglomerates like General Electric, companies realize that while accounting procedures remain the same, the rest of "how to do business" is "up for grabs." The idea of building the operation of an organization around closely-held core values has created a plethora of unique approaches to doing business. It is not uncommon for companies in the same line of business to operate their businesses far differently from each other – each having their own style. Consequently, leaders today feel that they are the ones best-suited to teach an employee how business should be done in their particular shop. Some may even have their own education process for incoming workers. I know of one very successful real estate firm, for example, who first "unlearns" its new employees from their former way of doing business before it re-educates them in the processes embraced by the company that now employs them. Whether there is a formal education system in a business or organization or not, leaders feel that they know how to run their business, organization, institution and they are looking for employees who are willing to learn, not just at the point of entry but at every level.

Do not overlook this point; being teachable is critically important to leaders. Not only is it among the seven traits of people who get ahead, many of the leaders I surveyed put being teachable in their top three! One even said, "If I had to choose between intelligence and teachability, I'd take teachability." Why? The answer is simple, you can always add knowledge, but you can't always add character. Stubborn people or "know-it-alls" are universally disliked by leaders in the workplace. That is a strong statement; but think about it. Those who can't be told can't be directed. Consequently, they work for themselves. If they work for themselves, they certainly don't work for the company that pays them nor do they strive for the goals embraced by that company and, that being the case, they certainly don't work for the boss immediately over them either – the one who is mostly likely to determine whether or not said employee gets promoted. Pride, arrogance, stubbornness, and independence are all the antithesis of being teachable.

It should be noted that employers today are looking for teachability right from the outset, even before the point of employment; they are looking for this quality in the interview! When a well-qualified worker sits for an interview with the notion that he/she already knows what is needed to be successful in the new company, it is more than a put off. A better tack would be to communicate that he/she has considerable experience in the field and is more than willing to learn a new approach to how business is being done in this new company. One highly trained leader said, "If a person has the basic skills and knowledge to satisfy the requirements of an interview, what will set them apart from others with similar qualifications will be their perceived or proven ability to learn the new job for which you are considering them." Note the words "perceived or proven ability to learn." That is the point – teachability. Some of those surveyed said that if a person is not teachable, they don't want them in the company – period. They will never get hired; forget about promotion!

As I worked through the material gleaned from the survey concerning this topic, two key thoughts emerged. First, employers tend to promote people who demonstrate a commitment to life-long learning. Second, they put people forward who take responsibility for personal improvement. I will deal with each in turn.

Probably one of the most important things an individual can do in any walk of life is to remain a student. The vast majority of the education we receive is gained outside a formal setting. We begin learning right from the womb and continue learning throughout life. We learn all the time – watching television, reading the newspaper, talking with friends and co-workers. We pick up information as we go through life. But, there is a big difference between a passive and an active approach to continued learning. Most of what we gain through passive learning is meaningless – how much the new centerfielder for the Cubs is being paid, how many years the crooked accountant is getting in jail, how many people try to climb Mount Everest every year. What we assimilate through active learning adds to the quality of our lives because it comes through an intentional targeted approach. An investor finds new ways to cut taxes because he subscribes to and reads investment newsletters. A runner cuts 15 minutes off her best marathon time because she adds speedwork to her workout schedule – an idea she gleans from a running magazine. A farmer increases yield by 10% because of information gained by following up on an advertisement he reads on the internet. None of these people would probably consider themselves students but that is exactly what they are. They are not learning in a formal setting nor are they satisfied to simply pick up tidbits of useless information as they go through life. Somewhere along the line, they made a commitment to remain a learner, a student. Their "studies" are intentional and focused – decrease taxes and run times, increase tonnage.

Let me add here that I am in no way against formal education, quite the opposite. I teach in a college training people for ministry. It is part of my life's calling and passion – training others. Formal education is important – vital. Education in many cases is the key that *opens the door* to advancement. In many walks of life you can't even get onto the "playing field" without the right education from the right school, much less "get into the game." I also know that formal education is not enough. Getting ahead in life requires the presence of abiding, deepening character and the continued acquisition of skills. Formal education is certainly part of the equation but definitely isn't the whole of it. I see this in my own field. Eggheads with education and no people skills are lost and often, eventually, unemployed. Teachers without tact have no audience. They talk and test but there is no real impartation to the learners who take the class for the credit, not the content. Preachers without emotional intelligence preach to pews where people used to sit. Those folks now crowd into the building down the street where the words from the pulpit are backed with the knowledge gained through formal education but made alive by culturally-relevant application, a cultural-relevancy gained through continued, focused, non-formal education.

Making a commitment to life-long learning, living life as a student, is a choice. Anyone can make it at any time in life. It doesn't have anything to do with our personal educational history, and it is not at all connected with our IQ. You don't have to be smart to be a student – just hungry to grow, to get ahead in some area of life. Like healthy eating and exercise, being a student makes us better people. Learning in one area affects our whole life. It makes us sharper and more attractive to others in life and in the workplace. It makes us more interesting as people. Life-long learners don't have to be the best or become experts; they just want to get better at whatever is before them in life. Moms who are students want to raise great kids, so they give themselves to growing as a parent. Leaders study leadership. They read books on it, maybe attend a few seminars. They even pick up things while watching movies, things other people miss, but their own sensitivity to leadership lessons enables them to grow in interesting and unexpected ways. Employees who want to get promoted and people who want to get ahead in life are students. They seek to get better at the task before them. The others, those destined to follow and stagnate, meander through life haphazardly embracing whatever meaningless factoids the mass media decides to drop on them. I have heard it said that when you stop learning, you stop growing and when you stop growing you are finished. That may be strongly stated but the corollary is certainly true; if you want to get ahead in life, if you want to get promoted, you must be a student.

The second idea is related to the first. Employers feel that the responsibility for personal improvement rests on the shoulders of the employee. The thought that, "I am the employee and you are my boss, so my job is to come to work and your job is to follow me around and make sure I do my job the way you want it done" is not going to cut it in today's marketplace. There is increased pressure on leaders in every sector dictated by an ever advancing technological climate that is constantly changing everything, from the way products are bought and sold, to the way wars are being fought. It seems everything in the marketplace is in a perpetual state of flux, and leaders need to stay on the edge of change to keep up with the shifts. The same holds true for workers. One leader emphatically said, "Individuals are responsible for applying their training to their current job assignment and situation. *They* must stay current with the latest changes in techniques and procedures for performing their job. Although we all may receive common training, what we do individually with that training and what additional skills and education we pursue is *up to us!*" One might respond, "That's not fair!" Maybe not, but that is the world we are living in and at the end of the day, the employee who takes responsibility for personal improvement and works toward that end will likely be the one getting the next promotion!

Chapter Eight Reflection Questions

1. Ask yourself, "Am I teachable, or is it hard to tell me new things?" Now, ask the same question to others close to you. Ask them to speak honestly to you.

2. What are the characteristics of a teachable person? Make a list.

3. What are your passions? Are you a student in those areas?

4. Are you a student regarding the subject of your work? In what ways do you demonstrate that?

5. Right now, dedicate yourself to being a student – a life-long learner – and purpose to take responsibility for personal improvement on your job.

Section Three

"Five Fatal Blunders"
(What Not to Do if You Want to Get Ahead)

I learned a lot about gardening from my father. I am no expert but he certainly is. He grew up on a farm in Michigan and to this day, at the age of 85, has a huge garden on a beautiful tract of land in South Carolina. In order to have a great garden you have to focus in two directions. First, you have to give the soil all the stuff it needs to produce vibrant, healthy crops – you have to maximize the positive stuff. Second, you have to do all you can do to win the battle with the bugs and the weeds – you have to minimize the negative stuff. Life is like that in so many ways. I'm sure you can think of some things that are similar in your world. In business, you want to increase sales, but you also have to eliminate excess costs. In war, you need to know your battle plan, but you also need to know your enemy. In cycling, you need to concentrate on your pedal stroke to maximize power, but you also need to reduce wind resistance and drag.

In the second section of this book our focus was the positive – you have to maximize the positive. But if we are going to be all we can be, like the garden, we're going to have to deal with the other side of the equation – minimize the negative stuff. This book would not be complete without discussing the weeds and bugs, those areas that threaten to hold us back. Please note: it is possible to have all seven traits fully functional in our lives and yet live life at a level far beneath our capacity, never getting ahead, always yearning for the promotion that never comes. Make no mistake; these fatal blunders are deadly. Not only can they hold you back, they can put an end to your career. From my survey, I detected five of what I came to call fatal blunders. They are:

1. **Dishonesty** – Trust is Based on Truth and Truth-Telling
2. **Rebellion** – Disrespect is the Father of Insubordination
3. **Insecurity** – Insecurity Stems from the Combination of Pride and Fear and Creates "Control"
4. **Self-Centeredness** – Stubbornness Manifests First in a Failure to Listen and Results in Self-Willed Responses
5. **Whining and Hanging Out With Whiners** – Your Attitude Determines Your Altitude

Chapter Nine

Dishonesty
Trust is Based on Truth and Truth-Telling

Luke 16:10, 11 (NIV) "Whoever can be trusted with very little can also be trusted with much, and whoever is dishonest with very little will also be dishonest with much. So if you have not been trustworthy in handling worldly wealth, who will trust you with true riches?"

In section two, I stated that the seven traits were in no particular order. That is not the case with this section. Of the five, one fatal blunder stood "head and shoulders" above the rest in order of importance. In fact, the strongest words shared in the survey were aimed at this point. In reference to fatal blunders, consider the words of one successful businesswoman, "Number one = lying. Enough said!" That sentiment was held consistently by leaders across the board.

Jim Carey plays an attorney in the movie "Liar, Liar" who has a problem keeping his word. The movie centers on the character's broken relationship with his son, who is living with his mom (the two adult characters having been divorced). Carey's character continuously makes promises he cannot keep and then lies to cover himself. The son wishes that his father would only be able to tell the truth and the wish comes true. The result is a comedy where the attorney is only able to say what he is truly thinking – no half truths, no partial lies, and no cover-ups. But the movie is instructive in what else is included under the category of a lie. He can no longer exaggerate or hide behind semantics. He can no longer give or leave someone with the wrong impression. He can no longer avoid the truth because something less is financially expedient. In fact, anything less than the truth is considered a lie. In the end, a hard lesson learned, Carey's character embraces truth telling as a way of life and the movie ends happily.

We have seen public officials and prominent citizens in the private sector hide behind carefully constructed shades of meaning to avoid loss or even prosecution. They claim to tell the truth, but later we often discover that so much has been left out that the sliver of truth they tell has been so tainted with false impression we have no other choice but to call it a lie. Creating false impressions out of partial truths may work in some circles, but dishonesty is death in the workplace. The average worker cannot call a press conference and hire a dozen wordsmiths to construct a statement designed to buy time so they can weather the storm. The average worker who gets caught in a lie is gone, canned, fired. Just what is a lie?

I think the movie "Liar, Liar" captures it well. A lie is anything less than the truth. A lie is also the truth shared in such a way as to leave a false impression. A lie is a partial truth or a half truth. Exaggeration is a lie. Saying what will be as if it already is, (knowing full well it isn't) is a lie. ("Yes, the reports are ready. I'll put them on your desk in the morning." And yet they aren't really ready now. You plan to work all night to finish them.) Simply put, lying is anything less then the truth.

One leader actually took the issue one step further, "lying, cheating, stealing, or even giving the appearance of doing so." If character is king, then dishonesty is the chief villain in the workplace. Association alone is enough to end your career. No doubt about it; dishonesty is dangerous. Many companies include in their employee handbook a statement that dishonesty and theft are grounds for immediate dismissal. Even the appearance of being connected with something dishonest is enough to permanently damage your future.

Many people play by the old adage that "all is fair in love and war." In doing so, some take that philosophy into the workplace. "In this dog-eat-dog world a man has to do whatever it takes to get ahead." It is not uncommon for workers to "play dirty" in an attempt to climb the ladder of success. But taking full credit for an idea that is only partially yours is lying. Shifting blame onto others to make yourself look good is also lying. Shading the truth to give a certain impression to the boss but leaving out certain details is lying. It would take an entire book to list all the dirty tricks played in the workplace under the guise of trying to get ahead. The trouble is, these things have a way of coming back on a person. When they do, they don't always surface in a way that the perpetrator of the lie is aware of. Often, bosses find out about some half-truth or dirty little trick and hold that revelation in their heart. Not wanting to lose a competent employee, the boss may never confront the individual outright. But when it is time to decide who gets the promotion, there will always be a "reason" why the dishonest employee is left behind.

The villain "Lying" has a cousin, "Stealing." Few would admit to being a thief for the same reason few would admit to lying; the definition is too narrow. Earlier, we defined lying as anything less than the truth. Stealing is more than taking money, whether it is embezzling millions or ripping off the cash drawer. Stealing is simply taking what isn't yours. One business owner put it this way, "an excessive number of personal phone calls or emails or social-izing on company time is stealing." The phone isn't yours and your time at work isn't yours. The company you worked for purchased it from you in the form of a paycheck. Taking lunch breaks that are longer than the allotted time is stealing. Coming to work late or leaving early without permission or without making it up is stealing. "Borrowing" ten bucks from the cash drawer or petty cash is stealing even if you do plan to put it back after you run to the bank. If your boss walked in as you slid that $10 into your purse or crammed it into your pants pocket, you could lose your job. For ten bucks! If he sees you but chooses to says nothing about it, he will likely never trust you again. All for ten bucks! Dishonesty is dangerous! Keeping inaccurate mileage records that are shaded in your favor is stealing. Taking work supplies home ("They don't pay me enough here anyway.") is stealing. Again, the list goes on.

I quoted a leader and made a comment in chapter four that needs to be repeated here. One leader said that, "Integrity is the hidden man – who you are when no one is watching." But the truth is, someone is always watching, and often we are unaware. I cannot stress this enough. Dishonesty is dangerous, deadly. Once your integrity is called into question, your ravaged reputation is almost impossible to repair.

One entrepreneur put it like this, "Trust – this is a deal breaker. I can train somebody I can trust. I will NOT train somebody I can-not trust. I will not waste his time or mine!" Trust is the currency of advancement. Where there is plenty of it, the opportunities are endless. Without it, your career grinds to a halt. But if the overall impression of your boss toward you is one of mistrust or even fear of dishonesty, your career is in jeopardy.

You may not like the definitions I have used in this chapter. You may disagree with my application of lying or stealing. Please let me point out to you that these ideas are not exclusively my own. They stem from my survey of 31 leaders, male and female, from varying career fields. Dishonesty is treated by them like cancer. It must be cut out, eradicated, destroyed. Anyone associated with dishonest activity, guilty or not, is suspect. This is serious stuff to employers.

Chapter Nine Reflection Questions

1. Have you seen instances of dishonesty in the workplace? Without naming names, list some? Do those involved know that you know about these things? Does the boss know? (So much for hiding!)

2. In what ways are you most tempted to be dishonest? What can you do to bolster your resolve for maintaining personal integrity?

3. Are there associations you have with individuals inside or outside the workplace that could compromise your reputation? What can you do to tactfully extricate yourself from those associations?

4. On a scale of 1 to 10, with 10 being the highest level of integrity. How would your boss rate you? How do you know?

Chapter Ten

Rebellion

Disrespect is the Father of Insubordination

Romans 13: 1, 2 (NIV) "Everyone must submit himself to the governing authorities, for there is no authority except that which God has established. The authorities that exist have been established by God. Consequently, he who rebels against the authority is rebelling against what God has instituted, and those who do so will bring judgment on themselves."

The verses above end with a warning of judgment for rebelling against authority. The verses above end with a warning of judgment for rebelling against authority. What does that judgment look like? Is it an eternal judgment he is predicting, one with fire and brimstone? Or, could it be a judgment meted out here on earth? Could it be a judgment directly linked to the infraction of rebellion? I believe the judgment is the natural consequence of rebellion; it is the fruit, the by-product. The two go hand-in-hand. Those in authority will always deal with those who rebel against them. Rebellion is an affront to them, a direct attack against their place of responsibility and authority. That is the way life is. It is no different in the workplace.

For clarity's sake, permit a short Bible lesson. There is a difference in Scripture between sin and iniquity. Many confuse the two and drawing a clear line here will help us understand the "innerworkings" of rebellion. Sin is a transgression against the law of God. It includes anything we do, think, or say that doesn't please God. Sin is primarily an action in the form of a deed, thought, or word. Iniquity is more basic; it is a disposition of the heart. It means to go your own way, to choose your own path as opposed to walking the one set out for you. It is out of an iniquitous heart that the actions of sin flow.

That was Adam and Eve's problem. God gave them a path to eternal life and it involved only one negative commandment – "Do not eat of the tree of the knowledge of good and evil." One command, one tree, do not eat. Eve, after being tempted, saw that the fruit of the tree was good for food, delightful to the eyes, and able to make one wise. So she took it and ate in pursuit of these three benefits. God wanted them to eat. He gave them permission to eat from all but one tree. God was into beauty. He created everything to be enjoyed. They could look at it all they wanted; they just couldn't eat it. God wanted them to be wise, but He had another pathway to take them there. Adam and Eve's first problem was iniquity. They wanted all the things God wanted for them, but they wanted them on their own terms. They wanted these things *their* way, not His way. Out of this iniquitous heart flowed the sin of disobedience, and they ate. The real tragedy is that Adam and Eve passed that iniquitous heart on to all of us. We were born with it. Right from the womb, we seek, at times, demand our own way.

Some readers, no doubt, had a hard time with the opening paragraph of this chapter. "Judgment? No way! Rebellion is our right. Buck the system! Unseat "the man;" I'm a free spirit." Nice try. But it will never work. Once you throw off the restrictions of authority, you become your own authority and eventually someone will come "under" you. And then the cycle continues. What you stand for becomes restrictive to the next group and then before you know it, rebellion is their right and you wake up and find yourself being "the man." One leader said, a rebellious person is "always fighting the wrong thing for the wrong reason." He is just trying to get his own way.

Iniquity is the expression of rebellion. Rebellion is in the heart of every person, but we all have a choice. What will we do with it? We only have three choices: crucify it, bury it, or act on it.

Which is worse, hidden or open rebellion? Most people would say open rebellion, and they would be wrong. Open rebellion is easy to spot and easy to deal with. It is the fool's way of expressing himself and judgment is often swift. Hidden rebellion is much more dangerous because it is much more insidious. It stays hidden and expresses itself in sedition, undercutting the trust of others toward authority and undermining the values of the institution. It seeks to work behind the scenes and masquerades as "one of the boys" in front of those in positions of authority. Hidden rebellion is more dangerous because it does more damage to the company or organization, and it often results in harsher judgment toward the individual. We use different words today, but the concepts talked about in board rooms are rooted in these ideas of iniquity and rebellion.

Two areas of rebellion were brought to light in my survey: disrespect and insubordination. The two are not the same, although they are related. Disrespect is an attitude. Insubordination is an action.

Disrespect can express itself in words or actions, but it is primarily an attitude of the heart. It is out of this disposition of the heart that the rolling of the eyes or the muttering under the breath comes. Some people are of the notion that they can hide a disrespectful attitude. But it is like a bad smell; it has its way of wafting into the room at the most inopportune times and in front of all the wrong people. Besides, bosses have "rebellion radar." They can sniff the scent of a disrespectful heart all the way across the shop floor. A person harboring a disrespectful heart can stand there and take the grilling, smiling all the way, thinking he is hiding his heart, but the boss knows exactly what is going on and wishes that right here, right now, right in the middle of this "dress down" situation the employee would say something stupid, so he could fire him on the spot. I have been there and likely, so have you. I have seen it happening to others as an employee, and I have also been the boss. There is nothing more infuriating than having a person under your jurisdiction who thinks he has hidden his disdain for your authority from you. Slight infractions of disrespect leak out, but never enough to actually deal with the person. One thing is for certain. He will never get promoted. And if he lives too close to the edge, he will be replaced!

Disrespect is like Tom Sawyer's hurt toe. Those who have it love to show it to others. They think they can show it around and the boss will not find out. I love the verse in Ecclesiastes 10:20 (NIV) (The insert is mine.) "Do not revile the king [boss] even in your thoughts, or curse the rich in your bedroom, because a bird of the air may carry your words, and a bird on the wing may report it." Note the sarcasm. Solomon knows that birds can't talk but someone will. Bosses have an uncanny way of knowing where the trouble in the unit is.

I had to laugh and grimace at what one business leader said about disrespect. She said that disrespect demonstrates itself in a "lack of self-respect, unkempt appearance, and a self-deprecating attitude all of which project a bad image. Take the Christian bumper sticker off your car if you want to act this way!" She is right.

Insubordination is an action that flows out of a disrespectful heart. One business owner said, "Insubordination? Fired on the spot!" While there is an indissolvable link between disrespect and insubordination, the consequences for each are far different. Often a boss wishes she had the grounds to fire a disrespectful person, but in most companies, insubordination is grounds for immediate termination.

I was not surprised at all to find insubordination on the list of fatal blunders, but I was surprised by the explanation of it given by the leaders I surveyed. I would have defined insubordination as direct defiance and the thirty-one leaders agreed. But they expanded its application to mean much more. One boss said insubordination is "ignoring the rules, failure to follow office procedures, failure to adhere to dress code or grooming standards, misuse of company equipment, ignoring basic courtesies and protocol with the boss, and not responding to instructions or directives." Before you react, remember that these are the people who decide who gets ahead and who gets left behind. These are career-makers and career-breakers. It would be in our own best interest to listen. It is obvious that some of the infractions listed above may seem minor, but since they are violations of clearly established and agreed upon policies, bosses often take such violations as a manifestation of insubordination – a willful act of defiance.

There are only three ways to deal with rebellion: Act on it – the fool's choice. (Go find a new job.) Hide it – it doesn't work. (Go find a new job eventually.) Crucify it – the only way to advancement. The principle of the cross is through death we find life. By killing rebellion; starving it; never giving it vent – even in our hearts – we position ourselves to do the greatest good. How foolish is it to attack the position we eventually hope to occupy! Once you are in a position of leadership yourself, you will be in place to make a positive impact on the organization and the people under you. Submit to the authorities over you, and work with them. Maybe they have learned a few things along the way, some wisdom or insight that you could gain by serving along side them. Maybe not! Maybe your boss is an idiot, a person wrongly moved into leadership. Rebellion is still not justified. This is your chance to prove your character while you pay your dues and wait your turn. The lessons you learn will make you a better boss.

Chapter Ten Reflection Questions

1. Define rebellion in your own words.

2. Does the state of your heart toward your boss or workplace bear any resemblance to your definition? If so, what can you do to correct that?

3. Do you harbor feelings of disrespect toward your employer? What is the root of these feelings?

4. What can you do to show support and respect toward your boss? List three practical things you can start to implement beginning your next day at work.

Chapter Eleven

Insecurity

Insecurity Stems from the Combination of Pride and Fear and Creates "Control"

Proverbs 18:12 (NIV) *"Before his downfall a man's heart is proud, but humility comes before honor."*

Proverbs 29:25 (NKJV) *"The fear of man brings a snare, but whoever trusts in the Lord shall be safe."*

The person who says he has no insecurities is probably the most insecure person in the room. Everyone is insecure at some point concerning some thing in their lives. We cannot escape it. The real problem with insecurity is that it is so hard to pin down exactly what it is. Sometimes we say a fearful person who avoids all conflict, stays to themselves, always tries to blend into the scenery, who won't look you in the eye is an insecure person. But we also say that the person who bursts into the room wearing a loud tie, boldly telling everyone how much money he made on the last deal, as if everyone wants to know everything about him, talking perpetually at a mile-a-minute is an insecure person. Both may be, but they are complete opposites.

And since we have a hard time pinning it down, we have an even harder time finding the prescription for its cure. What is an insecure person to do who desires to change? Should they attempt to become more conversant? That might work for the person in the first example but would only serve to exacerbate the problem in the second. Perhaps becoming more withdrawn is the best idea. Certainly the fellow in the second example could use an internal governor on his personality, but this advice is the antithesis of what the person in the first example needs. We need to understand the problem before we can put forward a solution to combat it.

Insecurity is our instantaneous, knee-jerk response to something that threatens our sense of self-preservation either physically or emotionally. Some people live continually with a level of insecurity in their lives. I call that chronic insecurity. Others are aware of its presence only under certain circumstances. I call that situational insecurity. For example, many are intimidated by the prospect of public speaking and being chosen by the unit at work to make the final presentation to the boss may be an honor, but it is one that makes them feel insecure. Learning a new technology can make some people feel insecure. Situational insecurity is a difficulty we all face, and this is not the type of insecurity the thirty-one leaders in my survey were concerned about. The type of insecurity that causes difficulty in the marketplace is the same type that will drop the anchor on your career, slowing the progress of your desired advancement.

Some label insecurity as a form of fear. Others see it as a type of pride. In reality it is neither, but it is both. Insecurity is the child of pride *and* fear. Whenever insecurity is working in the life of a person, two roots are in operation at the same time, pride and fear; both must be addressed for a person to be able to deal successfully with the problem. Both types of insecurity, situational and chronic, stem from the same source. At some point, pride and fear become almost indistinguishable. A person preparing to make a speech, for example, might fear being embarrassed by his self-perceived lack of ability to communicate. The embarrassment is an expression of pride. Is the fear driving the pride or is the pride fueling the fear? Who knows? Each person is a little different. We only know that both pride and fear are at work. A sales person learning a new technology might feel insecure because she doesn't want people to think she is stupid if she has a hard time grasping the new material. Is her pride, not wanting people to think she is stupid, motivating the fear thus causing her to feel insecure? Or is her fear empowering her pride? In the end, who cares if she isn't the fastest in the office to pick up the new technology? As far as that goes, who cares if she is the slowest? The truth is her twelve year old daughter is the one at home who runs all the "techno stuff" and that hasn't hurt their relationship at all. Technology isn't what the company hired her for anyway, and as long as she masters the material in a reasonable time and uses it to boost sales, being a "non-techno person" will not adversely impact her career.

In the case of chronic insecurity, pride may take the form of an inverted sort of pride or a frustrated pride manifesting in what some might call low self-esteem. These people spend enormous amounts of energy trying to hide. You might think, "That isn't pride!" Sure it is, otherwise why hide. If there were no pride, the individual wouldn't care what people think at all. Pride is there, so is fear of exposure. They don't want people to see them for who they really are. The trouble is, in trying to hide their weaknesses, they also hide their strengths. Pride may also be more overt as in the case of the person with chronic insecurity who talks too much and always talks about himself. He feels compelled to weigh-in on every discussion and tell everything he knows. He always has a story that is one degree better than the last one told. He, just like the fellow with "low self-esteem" above, is driven by a fear of exposure. In his heart, he feels he is less than everybody else but has chosen, in keeping with his extrovert personality, to prove to himself and everybody else that he is just as good as the rest. But, in doing so, he puts people off. When they recoil from him, it only drives him to push harder.

Everyone knows people who fit the two descriptions in the last paragraph. I have chosen two extreme examples to demonstrate how insecurity works. But there are varying degrees of chronic insecurity and those who struggle with it have probably been uncomfortable with this chapter so far. Again, insecurity is driven, generally speaking, by a fear of exposure and pride, not wanting others to see us in our place of perceived weakness. Fear empowers pride, and pride promotes fear. The insidious nature of the problem is that others are painfully aware of your insecurity, and you probably are not. Those who perceive their own insecurity are those who face situational insecurity. Chronics suffer with an amazing lack of self-awareness in regard to their own insecurity.

Why is this on the list of five fatal blunders, it sounds like a personal problem? Leaders know that "personal problems" carry over into business because, despite the massive growth of the internet, business still goes forth on the backs of people. Therefore, personal problems cease to be personal. Outside of lust and stealing, insecurity is one of the most dangerous sins a leader can commit because it destroys the people he leads. I am not attempting to play psychologist and diagnose the problems of your soul. My point in discussing this struggle is simply to give insight, so you can get past it and move on in your career. I want to help you get ahead. Top leaders know that chronic insecurity is a major road block to effective leadership and will stop your quest for promotion dead in its tracks. For example, an insecure person is afraid to tell the boss what he really thinks, instead he opts for what he feels the boss wants to hear. He is totally unaware that his boss and co-workers see exactly what is going on. One leader said, "The easiest way to lose your credibility is to be a 'Yes Man.' The boss whose rear end you are kissing sees through you, and your peers know it." And again, "If you cannot be candid with your boss and employees, you don't have a viable relationship with them." Insecurity inhibits the relationships you need to build in order to be in a position to move to the next level.

Insecure people are not team players. As team members, they fear the team and are often uncooperative. People do not like to work with those who are insecure. Being insecure and being needy are proportional; the more insecure a person is, the needier they appear. They become energy takers. They cannot simply work toward a common goal; something of self gets mixed up in the project. In some way it becomes about them. "That was my idea." "I thought of that long ago." "I did that once." (To be interpreted, "but it was better when I did it.")

Insecure people make even worse team leaders. As team leaders, they destroy teamwork through their desire to control the outcome. The attitude comes through. "This is my team." "We will do this my way." For some insecure team leaders, manipulation is the favorite leadership tool. Unfortunately, it isn't a tool found in any legitimate leader's toolkit and in reality it isn't a tool; it is a weapon.

Wise leaders never promote insecure people, because insecure people damage those they attempt to lead. As the subtitle of this chapter says, insecurity "stems from the combination of pride and fear and creates 'control'." Wise leaders know that control kills and that control is caused by insecurity. It kills passion and creativity. It kills relationships and respect. It kills enthusiasm and initiative. Control chases the best players away.

Secure people can spot those who struggle with the problem despite their best efforts to hide. As with rebellion, the worst thing to do is to try to bury it. The only way to deal with it is to deal with it! Permit some advice:

1. No one is perfect. Stop trying to hide your weaknesses. Remember, everyone has their own. The winners in life are those who aren't limited by them. Every fitness club has its share of body conscious people. They normally fall into two categories: those with perfect bodies and those who are ashamed of their bodies – those who have arrived and those who are still trying to get there. The perfect body people tend to parade around like they are waiting for a photo shoot for the cover of some sports magazine, while the rest try to hide or at least cover the less comely parts. I remember a fitness instructor in one of the clubs to which we used to belong. She was strong, had a bubbly personality, and was very good at what she did, but frankly, she was overweight. Yet it never seemed to bother her; even at the swimming pool she boldly wore her bathing suit and never acted ashamed. I often marveled at how secure she was. She worked in fitness, in a world where perfect bodies are worshipped, yet she never seemed insecure about the fact that hers was far from the standard. She played on her strengths – bubbly personality, knowledge of her job, personal strength and everybody liked her. She was much sought after as a personal trainer. Do not focus on your weaknesses, but do not try to hide them either; they show anyway. Play your strengths.

2. Never take yourself too seriously. Look back over your shoulder at your recent past. How many times did you feel like your circumstances constituted a major crisis? How many really were? Don't feel bad, we all do the same thing; we get worked up like the world is going to end, and then it doesn't, just before we call the President to bring out the National Guard. When we take ourselves too seriously it is a sign that pride is at work. Add to that a set of circum-

stances that threaten our sense of self-preservation and insecurity is the result. Don't be flippant about it; do your best, but if you "blow" the speech, the news of it won't show up on CNN.

3. Abraham Lincoln said, "It is better to be thought a fool who keeps his mouth shut than to open it and remove all doubt." Don't talk too much; it is a sure sign of insecurity. The longer you keep your mouth open, the more likely you are to put your foot in it.

4. If you are prone toward insecurity and you think about yourself first, you will likely never move to "second." Attempt to think about others before you think of yourself. In fact, thinking of ourselves is part of the problem – it is pride. Andrew Murray said "humility isn't thinking of oneself in a lowly fashion; it is not thinking of oneself at all." Self gets in the way. Think "team." Think "serve." Think "others."

5. Do not fear people's opinions. Everybody has one, and they don't count for much. Instead purpose to live the kind of life that others admire. And remember, even our heroes had their own foibles. It isn't about perfection; it's about direction.

Chapter Eleven Reflection Questions

1. What circumstances normally cause you to feel insecure? List them.

2. Develop a plan of attack to deal with the pride and fear associated with these circumstances so you can effectively confront insecurity should it arise.

3. Take a sober self-evaluation. Are you chronically insecure? Remember, those who are, almost never recognize it in themselves. It could be painful, but ask some people close to you if you are. If the answer is "yes," ask them also to explain how you demonstrate your insecurity.

4. What are your strengths? Ask others for input here as well. How can you better play to your strengths?

Chapter Twelve

Self-Centeredness
Stubbornness Manifests First in a Failure to Listen
and Results in Self-Willed Responses

*Psalm 78:8 (NIV) "They would not be like their forefathers – a stubborn
and rebellious generation, whose hearts were not loyal to God, whose
spirits were not faithful to Him."*

*Jeremiah 7:24 (NIV) "But they did not listen or pay attention; instead,
they followed the stubborn inclinations of their evil hearts. They went
backward and not forward."*

*Proverbs 5:12-14 (NIV) "You will say, "How I hated discipline! How
my heart spurned correction! I would not obey my teachers or listen to
my instructors. I have come to the brink of utter ruin in the midst of the
whole assembly."*

Many companies outsource portions of work they for-
merly considered part of their normal workload. I wish I could
outsource this chapter. Who can claim not to be at least somewhat
self-centered? It is the nature of man! We all suffer with this curse,

some worse than others, but it is part of the human experience. When an author writes or a speaker speaks, he should write or speak from a position of strength. I write this chapter from a position of weakness, but in it I must be direct and tell the truth. Your promotion is possibly at stake.

The truth be told, "self" is the root of all of our problems. All of life is about relationships, and relationships are successful when the focus is on the other person(s). Words like "give," "love," "serve" describe the interpersonal connections that really work. These words necessitate an intentional orientation toward others and are descriptive of "energy-givers." When we turn inward and seek to feed or satisfy "self" in our relationships we become "energy-takers." We make withdrawals instead of deposits; instead of building up we tear down. Self-motivated attitudes and actions are disruptive and destructive, not just in personal relationships but also in the workplace.

Relationships – developing them, keeping them, building them – are central to the success of any business. Connections with co-workers, customers, competitors, community planning boards, county commissioners, and city officials are all vital in the operation of business in a locality. "Customer Service" is a relationship word as is "Human Resources." And not just business, every organization is ultimately about people and the relationships that institution has with those people – schools and colleges, churches and non-profits, museums and civic clubs, and governments and armies. "Self" is anti-others and, therefore, anti-people. In the end, "self" is anti-business or institution.

As noted in chapter six, team players are among the most valued commodities in the marketplace today. There is no place for "self" in a team environment. "Team" is all about cooperation which requires, at times, an attitude of deference. "Team" is devoid of the superstar syndrome; the strengths of all are pooled and the weaknesses of individuals are diminished. When the team wins, everyone wins. "Self" cuts at the heart of team by demanding to stand out, by demanding its own way, by demanding to win alone. Lasting success in business requires a pulling together of the entire unit to accomplish corporate goals. Business, at its best, is a team sport, but "self" only wears its own colors.

Self-centered people are stubborn. They want their own way, period. Stubbornness does not come in one-size-fits-all. It is found in all types of people and shows its face in a variety of ways. There is the obvious loud-mouthed, hard-headed producer who is tolerated by management because he gets it done. When complaints are made about him they are dismissed by the explanation that he is "old-school." Being interpreted, that lame appellation really means he has been that hard to get along with for as long as he has been with the company! Then there is the quiet lady in the office pool who smiles and immediately nods her head in apparent acquiescence concerning some change in format or policy. Yet, somehow the work continues to be done in the same way it always has. Her sweetness belies her underlying hard-headedness, which is reluctant to change. There is the manipulative guy who finds a way to circumvent or undercut to get his way. There is the lady who clings to the policy book like a weapon and uses it against co-worker and boss alike. To violate the book is to violate the "law," and she acts like the corporate cop whose job it is to protect the company from the violence of change. Underneath it all, she is trying to preserve her own comfort with established procedure and her place of power as the protectorate of "policy." The list of manifestations of stubbornness in the lives of people is long and varied.

The reference from Psalm 78:8 quoted above refers to the stubbornness of the people of Israel in relation to God. Note that the accusation against them is that their hearts were not loyal to God, and, in the end, they were not faithful to Him. That is because stubborn people are loyal to themselves. They were not faithful because they were not fully committed to God. Again, they were committed to themselves, and as long as being connected to God seemed to benefit them, they stayed with Him. But, when their own self-interest shifted in another direction, so did their loyalty. In the workplace, self-willed people feign loyalty to the company as long as their needs are being met, or their personal goals seem in sight. Ask for something that doesn't satisfy their unrevealed desires and that's when the flow of loyalty runs dry. Their inherent infidelity toward anything other than themselves begins to manifest. That's when the eye begins to wander in search of a better deal. Unfortunately, sports heroes of today have made such a lifestyle not only the norm, but also one to be admired. Hit 50 home runs or rush for 2,000 yards and all of a sudden you can back-out of the five-year-multi-million dollar contract you signed last year to negotiate a deal for more money. Forget the fact that you gave your word. Does that count? Only if character counts!

Stubbornness is easily detected. All you need to look for is one tell-tale symptom. Stubborn people don't listen; they hear, but they don't listen. Have you ever talked with a person who looked you right in the eye as you talked, but you could tell "no one was at home?" They heard every word you said, but very little of it actually got inside the brain. Every parent has had this experience. Every person has been on the hearing but not listening end of the equation a time or two. The difference is that stubborn people habitually fail to listen because they are determined to do their own thing. Notice what the Scripture says in Jeremiah 7:24 (NIV) "But they did not listen or pay attention; instead, they followed the stubborn inclinations of their evil hearts. They went backward and not forward." The sad result is that, in the end, self-willed people do not move ahead in life. There is a point where force of will can take them, and after that, unless they

launch out on their own, they get stuck. Actually, they go backward instead of forward. Or at least they feel that way, as employee after employee passes them in the line toward upward mobil-
ity. A failure to listen communicates disrespect. In fact, ignoring
someone is the highest form of disrespect!

Employers are very aware of the presence of the stubborn and
self-centered individuals in their organizations. If you miss the first
sign, there is always a second. The response of self-centered people
to difficulty, conflict, and often authority in general is character-
istically adversarial. They strike verbally at those who cross them.
Their responses are driven by their self-will. "I will fight to get my
way and fight anyone who stands in my way." The leaders I surveyed had a very low tolerance for this kind of attitude. To drive
with tenacity toward a goal is one thing, but to drive over people is
another. One leader said, I will not promote someone who "pushes
his weight around, pulls rank, or is boastful – arrogant." Another
classified a stubborn person as one who is "unable to be corrected,
defensive, independent, unbroken, and often antagonistic." It is
clear that although these people may have passion, it is generally
for themselves. They lack loyalty toward the company or institution, erode the trust of leaders, take initiative only to further their
own agenda, destroy team play, lack emotional intelligence, and are
not teachable. They are, in fact, the antitheses of the type of individual wise leaders are looking for!

The great problem is that a self-centered person is "myopic"
and always thinks of self first. Myopia is the medical term for near-
sightedness. These people suffer from "me-opia" and believe the
world should revolve around them. The sad thing is they are often
blind to their own blindness. One entrepreneur said that a stubborn worker suffers from "a lack of self-awareness." How ironic!
So self-absorbed but so self-unaware! They often cannot see it in
themselves, and since they are characterized by a failure to listen,

they rarely heed the input of others. Worse, they cannot understand why, at times, others recoil from them.

Make no mistake about it; self-centered people will not go far
in the employment of others. Bottom line, if you can't be told,
you aren't getting promoted. The Book of Proverbs calls that person a fool!

Chapter Twelve Reflection Questions

1. All of us are somewhat self-centered and stubborn. In what areas of your life do you see this the most?

2. Since we do not often clearly see the areas in our own lives where we are self-centered, ask someone close to you to point out some of those areas to you. (Remember, your response to their input says a lot about who you are!)

3. What is the difference between having drive and being stubborn?

4. Under what circumstances do you tend not to listen?

Chapter Thirteen

Whining and Hanging Out With Whiners
Your Attitude Determines Your Altitude

Numbers 14:26-29(a) "And the LORD spoke to Moses and Aaron, saying, "How long shall I bear with this evil congregation who complain against Me? I have heard the complaints which the children of Israel make against Me. Say to them, 'As I live,' says the LORD, 'just as you have spoken in My hearing, so I will do to you: The carcasses of you who have complained against Me shall fall in this wilderness."

Ecclesiastes 10:20 (NIV) "Do not revile the king even in your thoughts, or curse the rich in your bedroom, because a bird of the air may carry your words, and a bird on the wing may report what you say."

There are so few things in life we can actually control. You can't determine how tall you will turn out to be – despite lying in your bed as a young teen stretching to make your toes touch the foot of the bed while you cry out to God to miraculously add inches. Even though you can temporarily straighten your hair with a flat iron, you can't convert it from curly to straight. One good rain or a good night's sleep and it reverts to form. You can't control who your parents are, and they can't control who comes forth from the womb. You can buy almost anything at Wal-Mart, but they don't sell IQ points. Most of life is out of our control, but there is one thing you can control and as it turns out, it is one of the most important things in life – your attitude.

Your attitude determines how you feel; it governs what you say; it dictates what you do and how you do it. Your attitude sets the course of your life, and in many ways, is the deciding factor in how far you climb the ladder of promotion – because your attitude determines your altitude.

God told the people of Israel that He would deliver them into the Promised Land. How do you think the land got its name? God promised it to them just like He promised to get them out of Egypt; just like He promised to take care of them on the journey; just like He promised to turn slaves into a great nation. God had always fulfilled His promise. And now, He was about to take them into the Land.

To prepare for the crossing into the land Moses sent spies to gather information and to bring back a report on the condition of the land and its inhabitants. Unfortunately, ten of the twelve spies brought back a bad report. Yes, the land was a great land flowing with incredible bounty but there were also giants, formidable enemies in the land, living in walled cities. The ten decided that the task was too dangerous, and they should abort the plan and find some other place to call their own. Go backward and live in already conquered territory. The other two spies remembered God's faithfulness to fulfill His promises. They remembered the impossibility of the former circumstances they had faced and how God had overcome them on their behalf. These two pleaded with the people not to listen to the naysayers. But, the people would have none of it, and they grumbled in their hearts. As soon as their attitudes went bad, their mouths began to complain, and their actions turned from heroic (as they had been in past campaigns) to cowardly. It is amazing how important that attitude is! As a result, God told them (paraphrased), "As you have said in your hearts, so it shall be." In other words, "Your attitude determines your altitude, and you have gone as far as you can go!"

The people recoiled because they thought they might die in pursuit of the promise and that is exactly what happened. But no giant killed them. Instead, they wandered for forty years in the wilderness, slowly dying off until only the two spies remained of the generation who grumbled. What killed them? Their attitudes! They grumbled in their hearts. Then they whined with their mouths. Then their actions became disobedient, and they withdrew, rebelled.

Notice, God did not rebuke them for the wrestling they did in their hearts. It is when they made the wrong choice and let those sounds out of their mouths – grumbling in their hearts became whining with their mouths. It was the complaining that drew His ire. God knew what was in their hearts – that was no surprise to Him. Notice in the verses from Numbers quoted above that the word "complain" is used three times. In the end, whiners always end up killing themselves.

We all face difficulty. "Trouble" is an equal opportunity visitor. Every person stands on even ground in that regard, from the oldest to the youngest, from the wealthiest to the poorest, from the CEO to the newest employee on the dock. It isn't trouble or stress that is the issue. It is how we handle it. Just like Israel, we all grumble in our hearts sometimes. Make no mistake, even the CEO sometimes wonders what she is "doing in this place," wishes she could get out, and wonders if it will ever change. People at the top level are not impervious to pressure. In fact, just the opposite pressure, trouble, and stress are chief components that make up the environment they live in everyday. We all face it, period.

But what comes next determines where we go in life. When we give verbal vent to the internal struggles and allow thoughts to become words, those very words are sometimes our undoing. Once they leave the mouth and enter the ear of another, they cannot be retracted, and the impressions they create or the damage that they do can sometimes have permanent ramifications.

A word of balance: we all have "safe places" where we can express ourselves without fear of harm. We need those "places" – spouses or trusted friends, a buddy who works for another company, a guy at the gym, a long standing family connection who is like a sister. These people become our "sounding boards," and the ability to speak freely is sometimes very important in the process of working things through. Sometimes, we have to say it in order to realize that we don't like what we hear. But, even in this, let these "sessions" be few. First, withdrawals are made when we whine. Whiners are energy-takers and whining is like pulling the plug on a drain. If you over-utilize the freedom to share, you can hurt your relationship. Second, whining carries with it a certain sense of re-lease, sometimes even exhilaration. "Finally, I can say what I really feel!" At times, we let the poor person on the other end "have it" as we vicariously dump on them in the place of the person toward whom the angst is truly directed. Be careful! Whining is habit-forming, and like an addict, we will go for stronger stuff and become bolder with it. Eventually, our whining will find its way out of the living room and back into the conference room where, after the meeting, we let one slip in the hearing of a fellow employee.

God knew what was in the hearts of the Israelites, but your boss won't know what is in yours until it comes out of your mouth. When it does, and there is no escaping this fact, the boss will know that you said it. As quoted previously, the Scripture says in Ecclesi-astes 10:20 (NIV) "Do not revile the king even in your thoughts, or curse the rich in your bedroom, because a bird of the air may carry your words, and a bird on the wing may report what you say." How do they know? Just realize that in the end, they will know. If you must whine, whine only in the "safe place." But whine rarely, even there, since you risk alienating those who make that place safe. And remember, whining is extremely habit-forming.

I tried to think of ways to soften this, but there is just no way around it, whiners are weak, or at least they are viewed that way. They appear not to have the intestinal fortitude to hold up under hardship. The trouble is, almost every complaint begins with some form of truth. But rather than mine the truth and deal with it properly, those who habitually complain do so because they coat that truth with their own personal sense of injustice. All of a sudden, the issue becomes about them – somehow they are getting the short-end of some stick. Whiners are typically poor losers – "terrible refs, the worst in the state!" They are lousy support personnel – "why does the boss get to take a trip to corporate while the rest of us have to stay here and slave away?" They even stink as bosses – "no one appreciates all the work I do around here to make this place successful." It is weak, and weak people make bad leaders. Even if he qualifies for the next post, a whiner almost never gets the nod. And even if he does, few will follow him since people do not follow weak leaders.

For that reason, whiners are losers. If you whine about your wife, you are a weak husband and lose ground in your marriage. How is she supposed the respect that? If you regularly whine about your job in front of your kids, they lose respect for you as well. Who wants a whiner for a dad? If you whine about how the game is going, some secure teammate will rebuke you, "if you'd stop crying like a baby and play like a man we might have a better chance of winning." I could go on. Face it, winners are not whiners! Do you want to get ahead in life? Stop whining! Whiners don't get things done. There is an old Chinese proverb that reads. "Let the man who says it can't be done not interrupt the man who is doing it." That is the attitude that will take you to the top.

There is more bad news. Those associated with whiners are often classified as whiners themselves. This is wrong, but it is simply the way things work in life. One leader cautioned concerning complaining and being a whiner: "Watch carefully you relationships at work; sometimes you are guilty by association." Be nice to everyone, but avoid protracted time with complainers. The "bird" often reports to the boss that "I overheard this person and that person talking." "I was in the break room with these people and she said." Beyond that, the company you keep reflects upon your own character. Why pay (often without knowing that you are paying) for someone else's bad attitude. If things go negative in the break room, leave the room. If someone is tries to include you in their web of whining, send them to the appropriate people to share their concerns. Why be classed with those of lesser character simply because they chose you to dump on?

If attitude determines altitude, cultivate personal vision. See where you are headed and focus on the objectives necessary to take you there. View hardship and headaches along the way as opportunities for character development skills acquisition. Let the junk that comes with life make you better not bitter.

Chapter Thirteen Reflection Questions:

1. Take an honest self-evaluation on this score. How much do you complain?

2. "Your attitude determines your altitude." How have you seen that operate in your own life?

3. Where will your present attitude toward work, toward others at work, toward your boss take you? If it needs adjustment, what needs to be done to upgrade your attitude?

4. Where are you headed? What is your aptitude? Make sure along the way that your attitude is in-keeping with your aptitude and not holding you back from achieving your highest potential.

Conclusion

Final Word

It is tough to end a book on getting ahead in life with such an in-your-face section. These last five chapters may have been challenging to read. The truth is, only the arrogant would fail to see themselves on those pages. I was convicted as I wrote. Do not despair, you can make it. This is within your grasp.

Face it; there will always be room to improve. Every step we take toward being all we can be reveals another level of change that must take place for us to realize our dream. Employers understand this because they encounter the same dynamic themselves. Most employers are willing to work with someone who really wants to improve. Listen to the words of one entrepreneur, "Most employees with proper training and mentorship can overcome these faults when they see that someone cares enough to help them fix it." And again, "I'd rather spend time mentoring a dud, than miss out on a real gem because I wasn't willing to invest the time in someone else who I felt didn't measure up. You never know who will really turn it around."

Let's make a plan. First, look over the "Seven Traits of People Who Get Ahead." Choose the one where you can make the most progress now.

Second, look over the "Five Fatal Blunders" and choose the one that is most glaring in your life. The point here is not so much progress as it is reducing drag, dealing with the things that are holding you back. Finally, consider giving your boss a copy of the book and asking for suggestions for improvement. Don't worry; it will be music to her ears. Remember, employers are looking for people who have the drive to want to get ahead. You are one of those!